Secret loves, hidden lives?

Exploring issues for people with learning difficulties who are gay, lesbian or bisexual

David Abbo

Supported by

Norah Fry Research Centre
University of Bristol

First published in Great Britain in April 2005 by

The Policy Press
University of Bristol
Fourth Floor, Beacon House
Queen's Road
Bristol BS8 1QU
UK

Tel no +44 (0)117 331 4054
Fax no +44 (0)117 331 4093
E-mail tpp-info@bristol.ac.uk
www.policypress.org.uk

ISBN 1 86134 690 5

David Abbott and **Joyce Howarth** are Researchers at the Norah Fry Research Centre, University of Bristol, UK.

Cover design by Qube Design Associates, Bristol
Cover photograph © Jill Rutherford and posed by actor from the Misfits Theatre Company, Bristol, UK.
Printed in Great Britain by Latimer Trend, Plymouth.

Contents

Foreword

I am very pleased to have been asked to write a foreword to this important report about the experiences of people with learning difficulties who are gay, lesbian or bisexual. This is a piece of research that is close to the hearts of all of us at Terrence Higgins Trust (THT) West.

We first started to target HIV prevention work with men with learning difficulties about nine years ago. At that time, we were concerned that men living in residential settings might not have had access to clear information about HIV and AIDS, and might have been putting themselves at risk of HIV through unprotected sex.

What we found, when we tried to do this work of educating and informing men with learning difficulties about sexual behaviour and practice, was that many organisations and individuals were not comfortable with the idea of people with learning difficulties having sex at all, let alone sex with someone of the same gender, and we encountered a lot of resistance to our ideas and plans.

Over the years THT West's interest in sexuality issues for people with learning difficulties has broadened and deepened. Broadened, because we do not deal exclusively with HIV infection at THT West, but with the whole range of sexually transmitted infections. We have a goal to improve the sexual health of everyone, whatever their background. Deepened, because the notion of sexual health encompasses far more than merely preventing infection, important though that is. For any of us, to achieve good sexual health we need education, information and other people to talk to about our concerns: people who have good knowledge of the issues and who won't judge or condemn us for our choices. These rights are also due to people with learning difficulties who want to explore their own sexuality and who may decide that they would like relationships with people of the same gender.

The definition of sexual health that we use at THT is 'the physical, emotional, psychological, social and cultural well-being of a person's sexual identity'. This is quite a mouthful, but we like it because it emphasises how important it is for a person to have the freedom to enjoy and express sexuality without exploitation, oppression or physical or emotional harm. It also highlights the close links between sexual health, mental health and self esteem. This means that research into the experiences of people with learning difficulties in expressing their sexuality must take into account how people feel about themselves and the extent to which they have been encouraged (or discouraged) by those around them to make positive choices about their intimate relationships with people of the same-sex.

The research reported here highlights the invisibility of lesbian relationships in the everyday lives of people with learning difficulties. It seems that at least some notice is taken of two men in a relationship together, even if the relationship is not well-understood or approved of. Two women wanting to have a close relationship have hardly any role models for their experiences and rarely receive any acknowledgement of the importance of their feelings for each other. These are not good foundations for developing someone's self esteem or self confidence about their sexuality!

Many of the lesbians and gay men who contributed their stories to this research told of difficulties in coming out, in having their sexuality acknowledged and respected and in getting appropriate support for their choices. A repeated and powerful theme is their desire (and right) to be treated like 'normal' people.

Many of the findings in this report are, if not entirely surprising, nonetheless shocking. Nineteen out of the 20 interviewees with learning difficulties had experienced harassment or discrimination for being gay – from family and from staff in centres as well as from people in the wider world. Feelings of loneliness and isolation are another recurring theme. There is talk of depression, self harm and suicide.

In view of the level of indifference, ignorance and prejudice that people with learning difficulties describe in this report, it is surprising, but ultimately heartening, that many positive themes also emerge. The determination and integrity of the interviewees shine through in their search for support and validation.

This research has already helped to raise awareness and understanding of same-sex relationships for people with learning difficulties and their supporters. Drawing on interviews with staff in a range of learning difficulty services, the report has highlighted examples of good practice across the UK, which can be used as models for organisations or individuals working with people with learning difficulties wanting to improve the quality of the support they provide.

An important part of our work at THT West is to challenge heterosexism (the assumption that everyone in the world is heterosexual) and I look forward to building on the partnerships established by this project to provide education and information to professionals working with people with learning difficulties. I also look forward to the empowerment of people with learning difficulties who wish to have same-sex relationships.

On a personal level, I have gained such a lot from THT's collaboration with the Norah Fry Research Centre at the University of Bristol and REGARD in the development of this report and associated resources. This research has uncovered much of what was previously hidden in the lives and experiences of people with learning difficulties. But I am sure there are more stories out there, and more challenges ahead, before this issue can be said to have been properly tackled. What we can all keep with us as we move forward are the words of one man, simply and clearly expressed:

"I suppose my ultimate dream is to be with someone who I'm going to be with for the rest of my life, who I'm going to love and cherish for the rest of my life."

Don't we all have similar goals for our lives?

Sue Peters, Regional Manager,
Terrence Higgins Trust West

Acknowledgements

First and foremost we are very grateful to all the women and men with learning difficulties and staff who agreed to meet with us. We would like to thank them for their time, welcome and thoughtfulness.

Before this research project began, Bristol City Social Services invited Joyce Howarth and Berkeley Burchell to do some work around homophobia and heterosexism in their day services. Thank you to them for some of the inspiration to do this work.

At our partner organisations, Terrence Higgins Trust and REGARD, we have been given invaluable support from Sue Peters, Victoria Marcello, Cathy Cole, Charlotte Simpson, Jamie Kinniburgh, Karen Shook and Kieran Bright.

This research project was supported by a committed and skilled research advisory group. Thank you to: Adrian Bakes, Berkeley Burchell, Jan Burns, Terri Cliberry, Victoria Jones, Seema Malhotra (who also carried out one of our interviews), Victoria Marcello, Sue Peters, Maureen Ryan and Karen Shook.

In addition, Iain Carson, Bryan Mellan and Paul Murphy provided us with information and support on very many occasions and Christopher Bennett, Hilary Brown and Richard Curren gave helpful input on some specific ethical issues for the study.

A gay man and a lesbian woman with learning difficulties acted as consultants to the project and gave helpful ideas and comments on aspects of the research. They would like to remain anonymous. Thank you to both of them.

At the Norah Fry Research Centre, University of Bristol we are grateful to Karen Gyde, Linda Ward, Fiona Macaulay, Paul Gelling, Julian Goodwin, Linda Holley and Alero King for their work and commitment to the project.

We are grateful for financial support from the Margaret Egelton Fund to carry out a small pilot study to look at the feasibility of doing this work.

Finally, thank you to the Big Lottery Fund for supporting this research.

Summary

Introduction

There is a growing policy and legislative imperative to ensure that people with learning difficulties are supported to develop relationships, including sexual ones. However gay, lesbian and bisexual people with learning difficulties may have additional needs or face particular barriers in this area of their lives, including prejudice and discrimination in the wider society, as well as from staff, services, family and friends.

Researchers at the Norah Fry Research Centre, University of Bristol worked in partnership with Terrence Higgins Trust and REGARD (the national organisation of gay, lesbian and bisexual disabled people). A three-year study, funded by the Big Lottery Fund, aimed to:

- find out more about the experiences of gay, lesbian and bisexual men and women with learning difficulties;
- explore what kinds of barriers or prejudice they encounter; to see how they have been supported (or not) by the services and professionals with whom they are involved;
- identify ideas, and then produce resources, for training and policy development that would enable them to get the positive support they need in this area.

About the study

The research had three stages:

1. interviews with 71 staff in 20 learning disability services across the UK about their views and experiences of working with people with learning difficulties who were, or may have been, gay, lesbian or bisexual;
2. interviews with 20 women and men with learning difficulties who were having, or wanted to have, a same-sex relationship;
3. the production of resources for people with learning difficulties and staff.

Findings: experiences of gay, lesbian or bisexual people with learning difficulties

First feelings and 'coming out' – Everybody told us about feeling attracted to people of the same-sex in their teenage years. The men and women we interviewed were all out to at least one other person. People's accounts of coming out were dominated by a fear and anxiety of rejection followed by a strong sense of relief if, and when, the news was well-received. Most, though not all, had experienced relatively positive responses from some family members. A small number had very negative reactions from their families. Those who had recently been through college said that they had felt unable to come out or talk about their sexuality there. One fear about coming out was that people might be asked to leave services or organisations that they valued.

Reflections on being gay, lesbian or bisexual – Almost all of the men interviewed described themselves as gay. About half of the women described themselves as bisexual and half as lesbian. Many of them had felt (and a small number continued to feel) that there was something wrong with their sexuality. People recognised that there were a range of issues around having a learning difficulty and being gay, lesbian or bisexual.

Homophobia and discrimination – 19 of our 20 interviewees told us about being bullied or harassed as a direct result of their sexuality. Much of the verbal abuse came from close family members. Many had experienced direct or indirect homophobia from professionals and four people told us about serious discrimination and harassment in their places of work. Half of the people we interviewed had been physically or verbally abused by strangers on the street or on public transport. Experiences of depression and loneliness featured heavily in people's accounts. Two men told us about trying to commit suicide and one woman had self harmed and thought about suicide.

Meeting other gay, lesbian and bisexual people – There was a fairly even split between people who knew quite a few other gay, lesbian and bisexual people, and people who knew very few, if any. The desire to meet and get to know other people was one of the strongest messages conveyed in our interviews. Most people had been to gay bars or clubs. Some had enjoyed this but others felt excluded or discriminated against on the 'scene' or simply did not enjoy it.

Relationships – Only a small number of people were in sexual/intimate relationships at the time of our interview, though most had experience of being in a relationship at some point in their lives. We heard accounts of all the positive and difficult things about being in relationships. One of the most positive features was having someone to do day-to-day things with.

What support do people want? – People wanted staff to be supportive and non-judgemental about their sexuality. We heard some accounts of individual professionals and some services doing very positive and person-centred work with people to develop

their sexuality or to help them lead sexual lives. However, we also heard many instances of staff and services that had been unsupportive or hostile. In practical terms, people wanted tangible support from staff to meet other gay, lesbian and bisexual people and wanted staff to see this as a legitimate part of their job.

Hopes and dreams – Five interviewees wanted to have children at some point in the future, although four of them said that they were being quite heavily dissuaded from this by staff and family members. Almost everyone else spoke about their hopes for the future in terms of being in a relationship.

Findings: the views and experiences of staff

Approaching work on sex and sexuality – In most services, the issues of sex, sexuality and relationships were not introduced into groups, activities or plans unless service users actively brought them up. A small number of staff in a minority of services took a different approach and were proactive in raising these issues.

Barriers to doing work in this area – There were concerns – and some reticence – about doing work in this area. These related to a lack of experience and confidence, gaps in policy and training provision, prejudicial attitudes and concerns about the (potential) adverse reactions of other people.

Homophobia and heterosexism in services – The majority of staff said that they worked in services and staff teams that were not homophobic but which were fairly, or very, heterosexist. Heterosexual members of staff were unlikely to recognise that discussing their personal lives meant that they were routinely making a statement about their sexuality. Some lesbian, gay and bisexual members of staff had been challenged about their interactions with lesbian, gay or bisexual service users. Most, but not all, gay, lesbian and bisexual staff were out to some colleagues. Very few gay, lesbian or bisexual staff were out to service users, although some were.

Staff experiences of gay, lesbian and bisexual people with learning difficulties – The overwhelming majority of staff said that they knew or had known men and women with learning difficulties who were having, or wanted to have, a same-sex relationship.

Privacy – Staff said that there were few places where men and women with learning difficulties could go to have privacy together for intimacy and/or sex.

Women's relationships with women – Staff described women's intimate or sexual relationships with each other as largely hidden. Expressions of intimacy and touch between women were characterised as platonic and essentially unproblematic.

The gay, lesbian, bisexual 'scene' – We were told about difficulties for people with learning difficulties in accessing the scene. Gay venues were described as not particularly welcoming and access to transport and the views of parents and carers could be barriers.

Supporting relationships – There was some frustration from staff that they did not feel able to support men and women with learning difficulties to achieve their goal of being in a relationship. However, there were many positive examples of staff and services working in innovative and thoughtful ways to support people in this area of their lives.

Conclusion: secret loves, hidden lives?

Twenty gay, lesbian and bisexual people with learning difficulties took part in this research. It was relatively easy to find men to interview but we struggled to find nine lesbian or bisexual women with learning difficulties across the whole of the UK. It seems that women's relationships with other women remain more hidden than men.

The men and women with learning difficulties that we met told us that being gay, lesbian or bisexual was an important part of their identity. It was a part of themselves that most people wanted to develop more. Despite the barriers to doing this, people's stories about their sexuality were characterised by resilience and successful strategies for finding support. Love was a major topic of conversation in our research interviews and relationships featured strongly in people's hopes and dreams for the future.

An 'easy to read' version of this summary is available on the Norah Fry Research Centre website (www.bris.ac.uk/Depts/NorahFry).

Introduction

This report is about women and men with learning difficulties who want to have same-sex relationships. The material it contains is drawn from interviews with 20 men and women with learning difficulties and 71 staff in 20 services for people with learning difficulties across the UK. The interviews took place between 2003 and 2004 as part of a three-year research project carried out by the Norah Fry Research Centre at the University of Bristol, in partnership with Terrence Higgins Trust and REGARD (the national organisation of lesbian, gay and bisexual disabled people). The project was supported by the Big Lottery Fund.

About this report

This chapter provides a background to the issues around same-sex relationships for people with learning difficulties. It describes the research study on which this report is based, including the methodology.

Chapters 2 and 3 draw on, and explore, our interviews with women and men with learning difficulties. The chapters discuss their experiences of 'coming out' and responses from family, friends and professionals. Chapter 3 focuses on people's relationships with other gay, lesbian and bisexual people: as friends, partners and as a wider community.

Chapters 4 and 5 are based on our interviews with staff in learning difficulty services. Chapter 4 focuses on the approach taken by services to sex, sexuality and relationships in general. It looks at the impact of having, or not having, policies

around sexuality and relationships. It also highlights messages about the importance of staff training.

Chapter 5 examines what staff in services told us about their experiences of, and views about, supporting women and men with learning difficulties who were having, or wanted to have, a same-sex relationship. It deals with the issue of homophobia and heterosexism in services for people with learning difficulties.

Chapter 6 draws conclusions from our research findings and Chapter 7 contains recommendations for staff and services.

Background to the research

Why are we interested in the lives of women and men with learning difficulties who are having, or would like to have, a same-sex relationship?

While there is a body of relatively recent literature on the sexuality of disabled people generally (see Brown et al, 2000, for example), and literature on the sexuality of people with learning difficulties that focuses on their *hetero*sexuality (see Craft, 1994, for example), there is an absence of work that explores the feelings and experiences of people with learning difficulties who want same-sex relationships (although for a perspective from the US, see Allen, 2003). Work that does explore how men with learning difficulties have sexual relationships with other men focuses on issues relating to HIV prevention (see Cambridge, 1997a, 1997b) and sexual abuse (Thompson and Brown, 1997, for example).

The voices of women with learning difficulties who might either identify as lesbian or want to have sex with other women are hard to find: "a minority within a minority", as Basson (1998) writes. Again, while there is work that has explored the *hetero*sexuality of women with learning difficulties:

> Lesbian sexuality is one of the least researched and least understood forms of sexual expression for women with intellectual disabilities. (McCarthy, 1999)

Legislative developments such as the 1998 Human Rights Act and the 1995 Disability Discrimination Act have helped to highlight the often wide disparity in rights enjoyed by disabled people in comparison to non-disabled people. Keywood (2003) argues that the 1998 Human Rights Act may impose obligations on public services to provide support to people to lead sexual lives if they want. However, the right to make choices about relationships has not always been at the forefront of the agenda of the disability movement's efforts to secure civil rights for disabled people generally. Shakespeare et al (1996) write:

> Sexuality, for disabled people, has been an area of distress and exclusion and self-doubt for so long, that it was sometimes easier not to consider it.

Disabled people's rights to a (hetero)sexual identity and (hetero)sexual relationships have been recognised only relatively recently; there has been still less progress for people with learning difficulties who might identify as gay, lesbian or bisexual.

Multiple identities

People with learning difficulties often face prejudice and harassment in their daily lives (Williams, 1995; Mencap, 1999). Many of the features of this harassment compare with the experiences of discrimination faced by gay, lesbian and bisexual people (Mason and Palmer, 1997). So people with learning difficulties may well face additional discrimination when trying to make choices about their sexual identity (Davidson-Paine and Corbett, 1995). Family, friends, supporters and professionals may, or may not, support the right of a person with a learning

difficulty to have a sexual identity, have a sex life or look for a partner in the first place; but individuals may face added opposition if they are looking for same-sex relationships. There may be additional cultural and/or religious issues around the acceptability of same-sex relationships (see Baxter et al, 1989). On top of this, people with learning difficulties may face additional prejudice from non-disabled members of the gay, lesbian and bisexual community. As Thompson et al (2001) write:

> Men with developmental disabilities, often without much social or financial leverage, are at the bottom of the gay pecking order.

People with learning difficulties are more likely to be socially isolated and less likely to have close friends than their non-disabled peers (Bayley, 1997). They are further isolated by their experience of exclusion and a lack of support from both other people with learning difficulties and other gay, lesbian and bisexual people (Thompson et al, 2001).

Barriers to making choices about relationships

Shakespeare (2000) addresses the practical barriers to a sex life and relationships that people with learning difficulties are likely to face. Non-disabled people will have a much wider choice of places and spaces to meet someone with whom they might have a sexual encounter or relationship – college, work and social spaces. These arenas are far less available or welcoming to people with learning difficulties. People need money to feel comfortable about how they look before seeking partners and sexual partners; confidence and self esteem are important if satisfactory partners are to be found.

People with learning difficulties are less likely to be in employment and more likely to be in receipt of social security benefits than their non-disabled peers (Davis et al, 1995; Burchardt, 2000), which means they will have less money at their disposal for going out, for clothes and for travel in order to be with and meet people. As Davies (2000) writes:

> ... it is fine to be celibate and single, if it's by choice. However, ableism, body fascism, and economic

disadvantage are key social factors that cause many disabled people to remain single and isolated against their will.

Our research focused on the whole range of human relationships that are a part of being gay, lesbian or bisexual and not just sexual ones. Focusing on sex alone would miss important points about how, or if, men and women with learning difficulties get to explore their feelings and emotions about other gay, lesbian and bisexual friends and lovers.

An important barrier faced by people with learning difficulties in this area is the attitudes of people who live with, and support, them. Staff in residential or day service settings are likely to have the same (heterosexist) assumptions as the general population, that is, that people *are* heterosexual. So displays of same-sex affection may often be interpreted as problematic, threatening, or misplaced. Attempts by staff to work with people with learning difficulties have, as Thompson (2001) notes, mainly focused on the prevention of sexually transmitted disease, abuse and, for women, pregnancy, as opposed to empowering ways to have sexual relationships. Thompson (2001), reflecting on many years of working with, and writing about, men with learning difficulties who have sex with other men, acknowledges that the dominant agenda is still to prevent 'less bad sex' rather than to support people to have relationships that are physically and emotionally satisfying.

At the same time, some more open-minded support workers, including those who themselves identify as lesbian, gay, or bisexual, will have concerns about openly supporting people with learning difficulties to think about their sexual identity. Cambridge and Mellan (2000) note the fear of some staff of breaching Section 28 of the 1988 Local Government Act, which was applicable in England, Scotland and Wales (and was only just repealed at the time of writing). This prohibited the promotion of homosexuality by local authorities. They also note the absence of explicit support from senior management in this area.

Support staff may also lack the skills or knowledge to support people here. Jones (1995) explored the ways in which services for people with learning

difficulties did – or did not – support the development of sexual identity for people with learning difficulties who were, or might be, gay, lesbian or bisexual. Her findings showed that staff did not have the skills, knowledge or experience to adopt an open-minded approach to supporting the sexual identity of the people they worked with.

Policy context

There is an emerging policy and legislative imperative to address the needs and rights of people with learning difficulties in relation to their sexuality and relationships. *Valuing people* (Department of Health, 2001) is the government White Paper that sets out a vision for the future of learning difficulty services in England. Section 7.39 says:

> Good services will help people with learning difficulties develop opportunities to form relationships, including one of a physical and sexual nature. It is important that people can receive accessible sex information and information about relationships and contraception.

The National Minimum Standards for Adult Placements in England (Department of Health, 2003) lists relationships as one of its desired outcomes for service users:

> Service users can develop and maintain personal relationships with people of their choice and information and specialist guidance are provided to help the service user to make appropriate choices.

The draft Sexual Health and Relationships Strategy for Scotland (Scottish Executive, 2003) recognises the needs of people with learning difficulties to be supported to "express their sexuality ... in a non-judgmental way" (Section 4.34). The Review of Mental Health and Learning Disability (Northern Ireland) draft report, *Equal lives*, (DHSSPS, 2002, Section 5.12) says:

> Meaningful relationships, including marriage, and expression of one's sexuality contribute greatly to people's quality of life.... Sexual orientation and preferences often go unnoticed and undetected or attributed to lack of experience, choice or environmental influences.

relationship with at least one member of staff who had taken part in the first stage of the research. One woman contacted us herself having seen a leaflet about the project. One man and one woman who were part of a support group for gay, lesbian and bisexual people with learning difficulties were contacted by us. In addition, members of our research advisory group, and a number of professionals who got in touch with us having heard about the project, approached individual men and women that they knew, or worked with, to see if they would agree to meet us.

With a colleague at the Norah Fry Research Centre, we made a video to send to people to help them decide if they wanted to take part in the research or not. In the video, our colleague, an information worker with learning difficulties, asked us questions about what it would mean to take part in the research and what would happen at, and after, the interview. The video covered topics like:

- What will the questions be?
- Will I have to answer all the questions?
- What will happen to the information?
- Will it be confidential?

We then sent the video, with an accessible consent form, to the member of staff with whom we had a pre-existing relationship. The member of staff then took the video and information to the person with learning difficulties. In most cases the person with learning difficulties was able to understand this information by themselves. In other cases the staff member went through the information with them.

Once we had received signed consent forms back from the individuals with learning difficulties, we rang them up to arrange a time, date and place to meet. We tried to give people as much choice as possible about this. People were able to choose which one of us they wanted to meet. In the end, all of the women met with the female researcher and all of the men met with the male researcher. Some people said that they would like the interview to take place in their bedroom, the place that they felt was most private. We had, however, already decided that a bedroom was not an appropriate place to carry out interviews. So we tended to meet either in sitting rooms, staff offices or in our own offices at the university, when

people were able to travel to us. One interview took place in the interviewer's car. Three people chose to have a supporter sit in on the interview with them.

We were open to the possibility of meeting people twice if that felt appropriate, but in the end we met with individuals just once. Before going to carry out the interview, we researched information on available local sources of advice and support, including gay, lesbian and bisexual social and support organisations. We took this information along with us as well as copies of *Gay Times* and *DIVA* (a glossy lesbian magazine). We had a small budget available to fund a limited number of counselling sessions for any participant who felt that they wanted additional support after the interview. This was being explored by one woman at the time of writing. In fact, the people we interviewed were mostly being supported by at least one member of staff. Everyone that took part in the research received a £15 gift voucher of their choosing as a small thank you.

We interviewed people across a wide age range – from 22-59 years old, with most people being in their 30s and 40s. One of the women was Black; the other interviewees were White. One interviewee was a post-operative, transgendered woman.

In the interviews we used a semi-structured, qualitative topic guide which covered the following areas: words about sexuality; first feelings about sexuality; coming out; responses from family and staff/services; relationships; sex; harassment and discrimination; experiences of gay, lesbian and bisexual groups and venues; identifying support for the future; hopes and dreams.

All of the interviewees used words to communicate. One man used the words "yes" and "no" and combined this with body gestures to indicate his meaning.

We reiterated at the start of the interview that the material would be confidential unless the person told us about previously undisclosed abuse – either as a victim or a perpetrator. We also made it clear that people could choose whether or not to answer each of our questions. We felt encouraged that in several interviews people said that there were some questions that they did not want to answer. When we interviewed a man who used a lot of body gestures to communicate, we practised at the start of the interview how he would demonstrate if there was a particular question he did not want to answer. In the course of the interview he used this gesture to show that he did not want to answer a question:

"So when you were out, did the three of you have sex together?"

"Yeah."

"Where was that?"

–

"You don't have to tell me."

"No."

"It's up to you."

"Yeah. – me." [signals – close to chest]

"Yeah. You want to keep it to yourself."

"Yeah."

"OK."

Information from both interviews with staff and with men and women with learning difficulties was stored in accordance with the Data Protection Act and we explained to all interviewees about their rights under the Act.

Analysis

Interviews with both staff and people with learning difficulties were tape recorded and lasted between one and three and a half hours. The tapes were transcribed and the transcripts analysed following established qualitative analysis procedures (Taylor and Bogdan, 1984). This involved reading and re-reading the transcripts of field notes to identify major themes or issues. Using a constant comparative approach (Glaser and Strauss, 1967), emerging themes and issues were compared for

similarities or differences then grouped into broader categories. Themes were cross-checked between the two members of the research team and particular attention was paid to themes that appeared to be unusual or counter-intuitive. Themes were then grouped into broader categories, which formed the coding frame for analysis. This frame was verified by each member of the research team checking each other's transcripts for accuracy and consistency in coding. Drafts of emerging findings were also discussed with our research advisory group and consultants with learning difficulties.

2

Being gay, lesbian or bisexual and having a learning difficulty

The next two chapters are based on our interviews with women and men with learning difficulties. This chapter focuses on the issues that we generally explored at the start of our interviews: about people's first, and developing, feelings about being gay, lesbian or bisexual, about 'coming out', and the response of people around them. In this chapter, and all subsequent chapters, people's names have been changed.

Accounts of first feelings and coming out

All of the people we interviewed talked about feeling attracted to people of the same-sex in their teenage years. They were attracted to people at school, at college, on the street and to famous people too. Few people worked out words or labels to describe their feelings when they were young:

> "Well, it was when I was younger, I kept fancying my teacher at school." (Pauline)

> "Well, not knowing the word gay and homosexual, but when I was in my teens I had this strong feeling that I was, that I weren't one for the women." (Jim)

People spoke a lot about how they felt, at this time of their lives, that they were the only gay, lesbian or bisexual person in the world. As a result many people tried to suppress their feelings. Angelique talked about trying to "blank it out" and Stephen said:

> "I couldn't tell anybody, because I thought it was the wrong thing to be doing. At the time I thought I was

literally the only person who was that in the whole world."

'Coming out' is described by Plummer (1995, p 84) as the complex process of moving from one sexual identity to a new one – "momentous, frequently painful ... dramatically re-shaping the life route: life will never be the same again". Everyone that we met was out to at least one other person. People were more likely to be out to staff in services than to family members or friends. In most instances, people had thought carefully about whom they were going to come out to. Almost all the men and women had thought from an early age that they might be gay, lesbian or bisexual but, in common with their non-disabled peers, waited until they thought that they would be supported to come out or until they found a member of staff that they could feel safe being open with. About half of the men interviewed had come out by going to a gay pub or club.

Daffyd and Ann both described feeling that they just had to come out to someone in order to get support. Daffyd told us why he had come out to his community nurse:

> "Because I was low. I had to have a mate, that's why. It was getting me down. I was trying to kill myself. I went missing. They couldn't find me. I was on the beach trying to drown myself. I was that lonely. It's horrible that. It's a horrible feeling isn't it, loneliness."

Ann told a member of staff at her day centre:

> "I says to him, 'I have to talk to someone. It's been eating me away for years and years and years.'"

Stephen went to a gay pub to see how it would feel to be there. He had a positive experience and said it "confirmed it" for him that he was gay:

"Actually walking in there I was petrified. I think it was about an hour just standing outside thinking, 'Am I ever going to go into this building?' And then I thought, 'Ooh yeah, it could be the first steps to the rest of my life.'"

Coming out to family

Four people who had come out to close family had had positive and supportive reactions. The majority had experienced mixed or negative reactions, while a small number were not out to any family members. Everyone spoke about how nervous they had been about telling their family and their concerns that they would be rejected.

Mark said that his parents had been very supportive of him and that this had made a positive difference to how he felt about himself. Stephen had one of the most positive experiences of coming out to his family:

"I decided to tell my parents about six months ago. I thought it was going to go really bad, but it didn't – it was good. They said I am who I am, and basically they respected me for who I am. I was petrified at first. I just wanted to get it over and done with. I just said like, 'I need to see you tomorrow, come down to my flat and make some coffee, some tea or whatever and I just want to have a chat'. And it went down very well. There was a whole weight lifted off my mind actually. Like 20-odd years of worry about something which I needn't have worried about really. I think I decided to go up into London and got totally slaughtered to celebrate."

Mothers were generally more receptive to the news than fathers we were told. Jim's account typified this. His mother was not very happy about him being gay but was beginning to be more accepting. We asked him how his dad was dealing with things:

"No, he's very, no he's quite reverse about it. He's said it's sick, he said it's sick that men want to, you know, stuff whatever. And em, you know hearing about these

gay marriages in America. He don't seem to like that sort of thing, stuff and that."

People recalled that coming out involved a lot of very high emotion. Angelique said:

"When I told my nan, she didn't take it too well. She didn't like it whatsoever. I was crying my eyes out."

Several families tried to persuade people that they were not really lesbian, gay or bisexual and some decided not to make any mention of it again – as if the coming out hadn't actually happened:

"I spoke to my ma a couple of years ago about it. One night I was in tears, I was breaking my heart and my mum was wondering what was wrong with me, so I sat her down and told her. I said, 'Mum I'm gay'. My mum says, 'You're gay? You don't know what it is to be gay. You don't understand. You're not gay, you don't know what you are talking about, you're just going through a phase.'" (Ann)

Paul had come out to his mother, father and sisters. All of them had insisted that he was not gay. He had decided not to talk about it with them again:

Paul: "They keep saying I'm not ..."

Interviewer: "They say that you are not – that you are not gay?"

Paul: "So I just keep it a secret from them now."

Interviewer: "And what did you feel about that, when they said you are not gay?"

Paul: "Um, hurt."

Interviewer: "Right, so after that time, did you and your mum and dad talk about it again?"

Paul: "Never, no."

Pauline's mother was worried about what it would mean for her daughter:

"My mum said, 'Oh you got to be very careful', she said, 'because, you could get somebody, and what if you decide it's not what you want', and I said, 'I don't think I can do that, decide what I want', and she said,

'What if this person beats you up, what if they're cruel to you?', and all this and that."

Most people who came out to parents said that they thought their parents already suspected. Sarah came out to her mum when she was 16:

"It was like, not angry really. I was just like, 'Mum, I fancy this girl and I just don't know what to do'. She goes, 'Well if you are happy and the girl's happy then go for it'. My mum had already clocked who the girl was at the time."

Those who had decided not to come out to their families feared negative reactions and rejection. Owen was part of a family of 10 and did not want any of them to know that he was gay. Daffyd did not want his family to know either and was asked why:

"I don't know. Er, well when I was younger they were calling me a sissy type of thing. I always wear rings you know and my dad said, 'Oh you should have been a girl, not a boy', type of thing and then they'd call me sissy and things like that you know."

Angelique felt that she was trapped between wanting to be out about her relationship and the fear that her family would not want to know her any more:

"Because when I tell everyone that I'm going out with [girlfriend], then it's the reaction of my family – will they accept it or will they be saying 'We don't want to know you anymore' – which I'm afraid of."

Pauline was unsure about coming out to friends because she also feared being rejected by them:

"I was scared because I thought, 'What would my friends say?' But I haven't told my friends yet and I wouldn't tell them until I found somebody. Because if I told them, my friends, and then they thought, 'Oh, I don't want to go round with her', and I don't find no-one, I've lost a friend, ain't I? It's a bit scary."

Coming out to staff

Almost all of the people we interviewed came to be involved in our research through a member of staff. This meant that, in general, people were out

to at least one member of staff. On the whole, reactions from staff whom people had actively chosen to come out to were positive. Christine said:

"The support worker was the first person I told. She was quite pleased actually!"

People had thought carefully about whom they were going to come out to. Most people were only out to a small number of staff that they trusted – in services that they felt would be accepting of them. Jim had told the manager of the advocacy group that he was a part of and he was asked why he had come out to her. He said that he felt that the service was one that accepted diversity and promoted equality. This had made him feel more sure about coming out:

"The thing here, everyone's equal. There's no racism, no sexism whatever, so I thought, oh, I'll come out."

However much thought people had given to whom they were going to come out to, there was still a lot of anxiety about what the response would be and there was as much emotion involved as coming out to family. Stephen came out to a professional on their second meeting and was asked how it felt:

"... actually, not very nice, because it was the very first time I ever told anybody, and he helped me through that. It was a bit emotional."

Ben and his support worker, who sat in on the interview, told us about his coming out:

Interviewer: "Were you nervous or ...?"

Ben: "Upset."

Interviewer: "You were upset?"

Ben: "Yeah."

Support worker: "Then you asked me to talk to your key worker, didn't you?"

Ben: "Yeah."

Support worker: "And the key worker said that you'd basically told him that he [Ben] felt attracted to other men."

Ben: "Yeah."

Support worker: "And that you were very scared."

Ben: "Yeah."

Support worker: "And upset, and worried what everyone would think of you."

Ben: "Mm."

Interviewer: "OK. And what was it like telling [support worker] and your link worker? What did it feel like?"

Ben: "Alright."

Support worker: "It was alright in the end, wasn't it? You were very nervous and worried about it. You were worried that you might be asked to leave."

Ben: "Yeah."

While people's experiences of coming out were very mixed, there was generally some sense of relief at having been able to tell someone. Owen said:

"But it's come out in the open now. It's better, I think it's better that way. Won't have no worries then will you? You don't have to be sick or worry about it. It's best to come out in the open."

Coming out to another gay, lesbian or bisexual person was described as being a great source of support – it made people feel less alone. Mark became friends with a woman at his day centre and described how they came out to each other:

"She used to talk to me about things and she'd say, 'Ee, you know, I can't wait to see me girlfriend at the centre'. I says, 'Girlfriend?', she says, 'Oh at the centre, this woman I know'. I says, 'Oh you like her do you?', she says, 'Yes.' I says, 'You know that's called being a lesbian, you know'. She says, 'Oh, I have heard about that', she says. 'Yes, that's what I am', she says. I says, 'Well that's OK. I like men as well, and it's alright', I says. We're great together. She says, 'Oh, that's

wonderful' and that's when we got to be really good friends."

Although the overwhelming feeling that people had about being out was one of relief, there was a continued anxiety that other people in the future might be hostile. The not knowing how people would react was ongoing. Sarah said:

"I try and hide it because you think, 'Are they going to accept it or are they going to give me shit?'"

Of those who had recently been through college, no-one had felt able to come out in their college setting to tutors or fellow students. We asked these people if being gay, lesbian or bisexual was ever discussed at college and they said no. Stefan said he "just kept it quiet" because he didn't know what the reaction of his tutors would be.

Almost everyone told us about someone that they absolutely did not want to come out to. Sometimes this was because they feared an adverse, personal reaction. Susie said, "I don't think they'd approve – my mum cos she's religious". But often it was because they thought they might be told to leave a service or their home or jobs as a result. Paul went to a support group for gay, lesbian and bisexual people with learning difficulties without telling his family, whom he lived with. He thought if they knew they would stop him from going. Mark talked about why he did not want people at his day centre to know he was gay:

"They might start being funny with you, saying, 'Well you know, you shouldn't be that, you know, you're not that, you're just being silly man'. They might even say, 'If that's the way you're going to start acting then, you know, you're not coming to this organisation any more'. You might even get dropped from the centre altogether."

Ann told us:

"I tried to talk to my mum about it but she just blew up, and she said, 'If you go on and on about it, I'll take you out of the centre'. She was going to take me out of the centre and that, so I don't want to be moved or anything like that."

Pauline's concern about coming out was that she would be prevented from working with children in her church group, which she enjoyed very much. Her mother had told her that if she came out she would not be able to be part of the Salvation Army and that it would mean that she wouldn't be able to wear the uniform that she had been bought. Although Pauline did not want to leave the church, she was worried about how much money the uniform had cost her mum:

"My mum said, 'Oh my god, oh my god, you can't come out of uniform now, that cost me 500 quid'. I said, 'Yeah, well, you could advertise it in the paper and get half of the money back, because there are people who want to go in uniform and can't afford a uniform, so you could sell it like half price'."

Reflections on being gay, lesbian or bisexual

Cambridge and Mellan's work (2000) suggested that men with learning difficulties may not want to identify as gay, either because of the stigmas attached to this, or because they did not know the word. We had thought carefully about how to start interviews and asked people what words they used to describe themselves. However, most of the men in the study called themselves gay, and the women chose either gay, lesbian or bisexual. Some were talking this issue through with staff, often psychologists, so had had opportunities to think about identity and consider what words or labels to use in relation to themselves. As well as sexual identity, issues about gender identity came up in some interviews. Half of the women we interviewed talked about this. Sandra was a post-operative transgendered woman and Alex talked in great depth about wanting to be a man. The other women that talked about this said that they felt they should be men because they fancied women.

None of the men we met identified as bisexual; all identified as gay. A number of the women identified as bisexual, and some found this difficult to deal with. Sally said:

"I always felt it was a problem. I could walk down the street and have a look at all the people, at both sexes,

and I think to myself, 'Why can't I just be like anybody else, like a straight person sort of thing?' I felt like I was an embarrassment ... it's very difficult, because you get girls coming up to you asking whether you are a lesbian."

One positive reason for being a lesbian was seen by some of the women as being able to avoid men more easily. Sarah said:

"You don't have these bastard men trying to hit on you all the time and some men only want one thing off a woman, that is the three letter word and that isn't my lifestyle, it isn't my lifestyle whatsoever."

The women could describe, often in detail, the type of women they found attractive. They varied from vague descriptions to very specific accounts. Ann said:

"I feel sexual towards larger women, well built women, women with big boobs and well-built. I feel attracted to them, their bodies. It would be a larger woman I would like to have sex with."

Ann had a rich fantasy life, perhaps to make up for the paucity of her emotional and sexual life in reality:

"I'm going to give this woman a name. Her name's Karen. I dream about this woman. I dream about her. It's just a dream. That's all it is. I dream about this large woman, having sex with her, touching her, putting my arms round her waist, kissing her and all that, on the side of her face, on her lips, putting my hands through her hair, stroking her hair, touching her head, touching her breasts, touching her body all over, touching her stomach, even putting suntan lotion on her. I even dream about her lying beside me in bed."

There has previously been little known about women with learning difficulties fancying other women, and we were not sure if women would talk to us about it. Christine, however, commented about being out in lesbian and gay pubs some nights, that were full of attractive women:

"Got to put your eyes back in!" [laughs]

We did not ask women direct questions about the opposite sex in the interviews. However, women repeatedly told us that they preferred the company of other women over that of men. Often their view of men was very negative:

"I have had a lot of problems with them. I am not going to be horrible, but straight ones in particular, they just tend to use me like a trophy and it is not fair." (Sally)

The women who described themselves as lesbian were very clear about whom they found sexually attractive:

"I would hug men, don't get me wrong, I would speak to men, but that is as far as they go. If a man wants to have sex with me I will tell him to go away. No way." (Sarah)

"So, I wouldn't say I'm mixed, because I definitely don't want to get married to a man. I'd die. I definitely don't want a relationship with a man." (Pauline)

Some of the people/men in the study were angry at the way being gay was regarded by others:

"I won't have people telling me it's wrong – there's not enough people telling me it's right." (Sean)

"All homophobics think gay men go round with their dicks on all the time, but it's not that, it's sort of like loving one another, bondship and that." (Jim)

"Sometimes when I'm given the chance to be in my element, yeah, I'm camp. But when I'm not in my element then I hide ... people should be allowed to express what they are. We are people not animals, people with a voice." (Sean)

Daffyd found it very difficult to come to terms with being gay and felt that he was gay because he'd been sexually abused by a man as a child:

"I didn't want to be gay ... I wanted to have relationships with women and have a family type of thing and then it's like, it's ruined your life one way or the other."

Owen, on the other hand, asked a lot of questions in his interview about what gay men did – for a living, socially and sexually – trying to understand how to be gay and wanting rules to make it easier.

An issue that many non-disabled gay men, lesbians and bisexuals have in accepting their sexual identity is the homophobia that they have absorbed over time – the feeling that their sexuality is wrong in some way. Women and men with learning difficulties are no different in this respect:

"I'm thinking, 'Oh my god, I am a lesbian, I'm not a normal person. How do I try and go back with being straight, getting married with a bloke, having kids and a normal life like any other person who I know?'" (Sarah)

Susie described herself as bisexual; she was having a relationship with a man and a woman. During the interview, Susie talked about getting married:

Interviewer: "Would you want to get married?"

Susie: "Yeah I would."

Interviewer: "Would it be Jackie or John?"

Susie: "Probably John."

Interviewer: "What is it about John that you feel more settled with?"

Susie: "Well, sort of like normal, well, straight and the way it's supposed to be."

Being gay, lesbian or bisexual and having a learning difficulty

We asked people in our interviews what it was like to be gay, lesbian or bisexual and have a learning difficulty. Most people had thought about this and had interesting things to say. Stephen said:

"I think having a learning difficulty when you are gay, you've almost got two labels. You have to think which one is the less important one and I think for me having a learning difficulty is less important than being gay. So when I actually walked into the [gay] club, I didn't have a learning difficulty that night. I was a normal person like anybody else ... I know with my own experiences, if you turn round and say to people, 'Oh yeah, I'm gay, but I also have a learning difficulty', the gay seems to sort of like, it doesn't matter, people only look at you that you have a learning difficulty: 'So what does that person know about having a relationship, he's got a learning difficulty, he doesn't know anything'. I believe that people would only look at the learning difficulty and not the actual person inside, which does happen a lot."

Stefan also recognised this as a problem and also 'discarded' his learning difficulty label when he went to gay bars:

"People don't know I've got learning disabilities. I just go in as a normal person."

There were definite feelings of being excluded by other non-disabled gay, lesbian and bisexual people as Mark found in gay pubs:

"Nothing happens. Nobody comes up to you and says anything, or says, 'Hello', or, 'You're nice'. And you just know that's because you're different."

Sean felt isolated in a gay, lesbian and bisexual support group for disabled people, which he felt was dominated by disabled people with physical impairments:

"Yeah, there is gay and lesbian disabled groups out there but they're exclusive – you know, we're not included."

One significant barrier that people spoke about was an assumption held by some family members and professionals that they were, or should be, asexual. Ann said:

"You see like for normal people – don't take this the wrong way, I've nothing against you personally – you see normal people think people with learning difficulties don't have sexual feelings, that we don't have any emotions, but we do. How I would put it is, I am not a doll that works with batteries, I am a human being and I have sexual feelings."

Some of the women felt that their parents treated them like children in this respect:

"They just think I have not got sexual feelings. They think I have got a brain of a child and they think I just don't understand about anything." (Ann)

Ann had, in fact, been prescribed medication to suppress her sexual feelings which she did not like taking:

"My mum had to get me sex tablets to calm me down, and I don't want sex tablets to calm me down, to stop me having an orgasm and all that, and I feel I want to have an orgasm."

Homophobia and discrimination

Of all the people we interviewed only one man said he had not experienced discrimination or been harassed for being gay. Much of the name calling and prejudice came from close family members which people found especially distressing. Views were often really extreme: about gay and lesbian people being sick or needing to be locked up or killed. Pauline told us:

"My sister, the oldest one, she says, 'These people who're gay and that', if she sees a film, and she sees a man or a lady kissing and she says, 'Bloody weirdos', she says, 'they should be locked up and throw the key away.'"

Sally was close to her family but they disapproved of her sexuality:

Sally: "I felt like I was an embarrassment."

Interviewer: "Do you feel you are an embarrassment?"

Sally: "Yeah."

Interviewer: "Really?"

Sally: "Sometimes. Not when I am with the other people ... it is my relations."

Interviewer: "Your family?"

Sally: "Yeah, they make me feel like that sometimes."

Interviewer: "That's hard, because it sounds like your family are quite important to you?"

Sally: "Yeah, they are very important to me actually."

Interviewer: "And what they think of you is important to you?"

Sally: "Yeah."

Sarah was in a relationship with Angelique. Angelique's family had very divided views about the relationship:

"Angelique's cousins love me to bits. Angelique's nan hates me. She despises gay people: 'They should be shot.' I even heard her nan on the phone saying, 'Please don't do this to me. You are my grand daughter, I don't want you being gay. I do not want you being with that woman. It is either Sarah or your family.' It is very sad."

Common to women's experiences was friends and family members telling them that what they "really needed was a man":

"What gets me ... a couple of them used to say, 'How can you not fancy men. If you've never tried it, how do you know?' I said, 'Well I know I don't fancy men. That's it.' I mean it got on my nerves going on and on. He used to say, 'Well how can you know about what you've never had?' I used to say, 'Because I just don't [fancy men].'" (Christine)

With the exception of one person, everybody in the study had had experiences of staff being homophobic and negative about their sexuality. Sean lived independently in a flat that was located above a residential learning disability service. The manager of the service had no professional or personal relationship with Sean. However, she told him one day that he was not allowed to bring men back to his flat:

Sean: "She told me last week that I'm not allowed to bring a man back – to have sex ..."

Interviewer: "Who's this?"

Sean: "The manager of the house that we share. The whole block ... we've got the top floor to ourselves but the staff at the bottom are [x service] ... a residential ... community service. And they've started to muscle in and say things. She's the one who told me not to have a man there cos it's embarrassing."

Interviewer: "Why ... is she anything to do with you?"

Sean: "No, no ... sticking her nose in when she shouldn't be doing."

Interviewer: "And she told you that it would be embarrassing for you to have..."

Sean: "For other residents in the house."

Interviewer: "... for you to have sex with men?"

Sean: "Yeah. The way I look at it, if they've got a problem with my sexuality, it's their problem. She goes to me, 'Think about the three women's feelings downstairs'. 'What do you mean about the three women downstairs?' 'Well they've never had sex.' Well it's not my problem, is it?"

Interviewer: "How did this woman even know or find out that you're gay?"

Sean: "It leaked out by services – she read the file."

More common than this outright prejudice was staff showing their unease with the person's sexuality. Stephen said his link worker was "nice" but couldn't cope when he wanted to talk about being gay:

"There's one member of staff who's – she doesn't show it, I mean she's a very nice member of staff – but I know she has a problem with gay and lesbian people. It's obvious to me – she doesn't make it nasty obvious, you know what I mean, but if I want a one-to-one and I want to talk about, say my partner or a friend that I might be going out with, yeah, she'll try and pass it on to someone else. I mean she will do it at a very big push, but she doesn't want to be involved in that part of my life. It's OK, but if she's there to support me, she should be there for all parts of my life, not just for the bits she thinks are right for her."

Four of the people with learning difficulties who had a job said they had experienced homophobia in the workplace. Pauline had been told by colleagues that the Bible said it was wrong to be gay. Sean was called names at work:

"I was bullied at work. They called me faggot. They called me child molester, pervert. I was ... like my favourite colour is pink and they would say, 'Oh poofy pink.' After a while it got on my nerves, you know what I mean? The name calling ... to be called a paedophile. That was it. That was the last straw."

Stephen dealt with the homophobia from someone he managed at work by writing the person a letter that told the story of his life and described what kind of person he was and the difficulties he had faced. Having read the letter, the colleague apologised for what he had said and done.

These two people worked in advocacy organisations. Both faced outright discrimination – name calling. At the same time they were called upon to work on anything that had to do with sexuality. They were presumed to be experts on anything to do with sexuality because they were gay:

"What I didn't like [at work] was if there were any sexuality issues it was, 'Oh Sean will sort it.' I was like, 'Wait a minute, I'm not a heterosexual – how can I discuss issues about straight sex – you know what I mean?' It was like, 'He's gay, he can do sexuality'."

Half of the people we interviewed told us about being physically and verbally abused by strangers in their neighbourhoods and on public transport. Christine said:

"I'm a bit dubious of the kids, you know, like where I live, because some of them do call over like, and spat at us and stuff, and I hate that. I mean they are not as bad now. They lay off a bit now. But when I first moved they used to call over and everything, and they used to hit the ball at the door and everything, and chuck stones and stuff."

Robert and Paul had both been attacked on the street and neither felt confident that telling the police would make any difference so neither had reported the incidents:

Robert: "I've been attacked now, of course I was scared – they beat me up – attacked me."

Interviewer: "That's terrible. What did you do? Did you go to the police about it?"

Robert: "No. I just went to hospital the next day."

Interviewer: "Why did you decide not to ...?"

Robert: "I don't know, because I don't want courts involved."

Interviewer: "You didn't want the courts involved?"

Robert: "The police – they don't like gay people – I don't know."

Paul said that young lads on the street shouted names at him:

Interviewer: "What kinds of words do they use?"

Paul: "Um, like gay."

Interviewer: "Right, and how do you feel about that? What does that feel like?"

Paul: "Um, it hurts us."

Interviewer: "Yes, and do you feel frightened?"

Paul: "Yes. Yes, once, when they pushed me."

In the face of this level of discrimination, people told us about their coping strategies and how they tried to be resilient. Some people tried to reason with, or talk about sexuality with, others. Pauline was routinely told that it was against the Bible to be a lesbian:

"When I talked to my friend, I pulled her up on this and I said, 'Yeah, but I don't understand it, because I have read things in the Bible where it says we're all God's children. Now if we're all God's children, it don't matter if we're pink or with black spots, or whatever, then why can't we do that?'"

Other people had decided that they would "shut off" to the name calling or develop a "hard edge", as Susie called it:

"If you look hard they don't touch you. If you look vulnerable, they do. Horrible, you've got to be at aggressive attitude all the time. Always on the edge."

Sean, in common with several other people, described standing up for himself and being proud of being gay. However, despite this, Sean was conscious that if he was completely assertive it might have a detrimental impact on relationships with staff and services. So he stopped himself being completely forthright with a homophobic member of staff:

"... can't just tell her to bog off cos likes of me ... scared of having services taken away. So we're in a predicament where there's nowt we can do."

Abuse and mental health issues

Half of the men and women we met spoke about having been abused in some way, at some time in their lives. Most of these people had been sexually abused. One had been pushed in the street for being gay, another had been beaten up more than once in homophobic attacks as well as being sexually assaulted. We did not specifically ask about sexual assaults. People spoke about them because they were still affecting their lives in some way:

"I am getting there slowly, but I can't really say that I have forgiven the person who has done that to me. I can't really say that I want to, because at the end of the day, he nearly messed up my life to be honest." (Sarah)

Some people had been sexually assaulted as children. For others, the abuse was much more recent. In trying to understand why they were gay, lesbian or bisexual, some of the people made links with their experience of being abused:

"I was abused when I was a child. I think that's put me off of men anyway." (Pauline)

Daffyd: "And I didn't want to be gay type of thing, but it's too late now, I am."

Interviewer: "So do you think that's why, do you think you're gay because that [sexual abuse as a child] happened?"

Daffyd: "Yeah."

On the other hand, Sean felt that it wasn't right to link the two things:

"People say to me, and this is another thing I get annoyed about, 'How can you be gay when you've been abused by men?' But I don't think that comes into it, into what your feeling is. What he did to me was wrong – it was not consenting, it was wrong."

MIND reported in 2003 that two thirds of gay men, lesbians and bisexuals in the general population experience mental ill health at some time in their lives. The people we met talked about loneliness, isolation and depression in quite a lot of detail. They had for many years felt as if they were the only gay or lesbian person in the world. Time and again people told us that they had no-one else to talk to about how they felt. Two men spoke to us of having tried to commit suicide and one woman had self harmed and thought about suicide. Ann spoke at length about her depression and pain at feeling isolated and the fact that her family wouldn't listen to, or support, her:

"I am isolated and I am lonely and I just feel my family doesn't understand how I feel and you are so lonely. I am just, oh god, there's a person in here that's crying and my heart has been broken, but I try to put a brave face on it for my family's sake. It does wind me up. It makes me so angry and so frustrated. Why am I getting punished, why am I having the life of a child instead of an adult?"

Summary

- *First feelings and 'coming out'* – Everybody told us about feeling attracted to people of the same-sex in their teenage years. The men and women we interviewed were all out to at least one other person. They were more likely to have come out to staff members, though most had also come out to close family members and friends. People's accounts of coming out were dominated by a fear of rejection, followed by a strong sense of relief if the news was well received. Most, though not all, had experienced relatively positive responses from some family members; a small number had very negative reactions. In terms of coming out to staff, our interviewees had thought very carefully about whom exactly they were going to tell. Even after coming out, people were conscious that they could not guarantee how other people would react in the future. Those who had recently been through college said that they had felt unable to come out or talk about their sexuality there. One fear about coming out was that people might be asked to leave services or organisations that they valued as a result.

- *Reflections on being gay, lesbian or bisexual* – Almost all of the men interviewed described themselves as gay. About half of the women described themselves as bisexual and half as lesbian. Many of them had felt (and a small number continued to feel) that there was something wrong with their sexuality. People recognised that there were issues around having a learning difficulty and being gay, lesbian or bisexual. Some men said they 'dropped' their learning difficulty 'label' when they were in gay places like bars. Some men and women felt that it meant they faced additional discrimination from families, staff and the wider non-disabled gay, lesbian and bisexual community.

- *Homophobia and discrimination* – 19 of our 20 interviewees told us about being bullied or harassed as a direct result of their sexuality. Much of the verbal abuse came from close family members. Many had experienced direct or indirect homophobia from professionals and four people told us about serious discrimination and harassment in their places of work. Half of the people we interviewed had been physically or verbally abused by strangers on the street or on public transport.

- *Abuse and mental health* – One half of our interviewees had been sexually abused at some point in their lives. Three people made links between these experiences of abuse and their sexuality. Accounts of isolation, loneliness and depression featured heavily in people's descriptions of their lives.

3

Finding a place in the world: belonging, love, sex and dreams

This chapter explores a whole range of relationships that we talked about in our interviews with women and men with learning difficulties: relationships with other gay, lesbian and bisexual people and hopes for future relationships; connections with a wider gay, lesbian and bisexual community; and relationships with staff and services. It concludes with accounts of people's hopes and dreams for their futures.

Sarah and Angelique: a love story

"I didn't want to be lonely, you know and so I had a word with my mum and to be honest it was mostly my mum's idea to go and find someone else, so I looked to my mum to be honest. I left an advert in this magazine. I just said that I was looking for someone and hopefully a friendship at first and then a relationship. About a couple of weeks later I had two messages and they were from Angelique. At the time she just wanted a friend, but for me it was love at first sight." (Sarah)

"I think she said she'd put an ad in the magazine and I looked in it cos at that time I was just looking for a friend. So I rang up and left a message and the next Tuesday she got back to me and started talking and then we met up the day after. And we just walked around town, we were just walking about town, flirting, having a laugh and at that time I was still trying to hide it that I really liked her, but I knew that she liked me a lot. It was really fun. Sitting down, have something to eat. We just laughed and talked. It was just different from meeting a male who wanted something different from going into a woman who was wanting to talk. She gave me a kiss and I didn't want to go ..." (Angelique)

Meeting and knowing other gay, lesbian or bisexual people

The men and women we met had different experiences of meeting other gay, lesbian and bisexual people, from Angelique, who had "loads of lesbian friends and gay male friends as well", to Ann who said:

"I don't know if anybody is a lesbian down at the [day] centre. I don't know of any other lesbians, not to my knowledge anyway."

Most people had met at least one other person who identified as gay, lesbian or bisexual. They always saw this as a positive part of their life, breaking down the isolation people had felt at one time. Stephen talked with a support worker who was gay, and said why it was good to talk to him:

"Because he's gay. It's talking to another gay person about the same pile of issues, that's the main thing for me. I know at some stage in his life, the experiences I'm going through, he's been through as well."

Stephen was unusual in having an 'out' professional to talk with. Others met gay, lesbian and bisexual people through going to pubs, support groups or, for Stefan, through telephone chatlines. Support groups, often open to anyone, were generally viewed positively. Mark went to one for young gay men:

"I went there for about seven years and it used to be really nice there and they kind of understood that I had a problem and they don't mind that. And some of them got on really well with me, but then last July, when I was 25, I had to leave there because I was too old."

Mark then found one of the rare groups for gay, lesbian and bisexual people with learning difficulties, which he said was:

"Good. It was nice to be around people with learning problems who were the same as you."

Paul, on the other hand, described a group that was not specifically for disabled people as "a bit separate" and didn't really make friends there. Despite this he said he quite liked going.

However, for those who did not find another gay, lesbian or bisexual person to talk to, Ann's experience of loneliness and isolation was common:

"Nobody to talk to and that's what hurts the most. That's why I would like to go to another lesbian woman to talk to her about it. Somebody who I feel who understands where I am coming from."

Pubs, clubs and the 'scene'

Most of the people we met had experienced the 'gay scene' in some way. This varied from just one visit to regularly clubbing, or using other gay establishments. For Sarah and Angelique, this had been a very positive experience:

"The gay scene is just amazing, an amazing atmosphere." (Sarah)

"We go down to a nightclub. We go down there every Thursday just to see our mates, to relax and have a laugh." (Angelique)

Christine talked about the pubs in town being really good:

"When we go out, we like cuddle and that's because people aren't as ... they are all gay people so they do the same thing. You don't feel as isolated."

She also talked a lot about going to the local Pride (gay festival), which took place that weekend. She had been going for three years and enjoyed it immensely:

"It was good, it's like, it's just like because everyone's dead friendly with each other."

Jim had recently used a local sauna for the first time and was very pleased with finding men there to have sex with. Owen had visited a gay pub:

"I went up to the bar and someone asked me if I wanted a drink and go dancing with them. It were great."

However, not all experiences were this positive. For Sean, it was another experience of discrimination:

Sean: "When I came out I went to the village [gay district]. Saturday night it was. And he went, 'You're not gay enough'."

Interviewer: "Who said that?"

Sean: "The bouncers. So I said, 'Alright, well what do I have to do? Kiss somebody to get in?' So I stood back and they let all these straight men in – discrimination – you know what I mean. It's the image – if we don't fit the slim, good looking, able, we don't fit in."

In the end Sean was able to go to one bar in the city where the bouncer was friendly. But when the bouncer moved to another pub, Sean would have to change pub too. "It's not fair to limit us down to one bar", he said.

Mark and Paul hadn't experienced this level of prejudice, but still felt they were excluded:

"I've been to a gay pub, but nothing happens, nobody comes up to you and says anything, or says, 'Hello', or, 'You're nice', or just ... all go about their own business. And you just say, well you know, you just know that's because you know that you're different." (Mark)

Interviewer: "When you go to the pub, does your group like sit together?"

Paul: "Um yes."

Interviewer: "And do other people from outside the group come over and talk, or do you go and talk to other people in the pub or ..."

Paul: "Uh no, we just talk between ourselves."

Interviewer: "Right, and do you like that, or would you like to talk to other people in the pub?"

Paul: "Talk to other people in the pub."

Many of those who had been to gay scene venues did so with support from a professional. However, Pauline had tried to go by herself, as she had no-one willing to support her:

"I nearly walked there the other day. It was so sunny and all these people were out there under the umbrellas with the tables, and a part of me wanted to go there and a part of me was two steps back. I will try and get there, but … I know it's scary, very scary."

Love, sex and relationships

People told us about all kinds of relationships – sexual, non-sexual, past loves, new affairs, current crushes. Sean told us about a man he liked in the support group he attended:

"I would like to have a relationship with him. When he comes to the group he always says he's looking forward to seeing me. And that sort of things, that's nice when he says that. He comes out with some belters – you know, he says to me, 'If I kissed you, I'd never let you go'. That's nice."

While only a small number of people that we met were in relationships at the time of the interview, others had had relationships in the past. Like all relationships, some had been complex and difficult as well as exciting. Owen said he'd fallen in love with a boy at school but that when the head teacher found out the boy had to leave the school:

"… that boy left, I never saw him again. That broke my heart then. Because the other boy was unhappy, you know, at home and he came to me see, for love and things like that, and that's what he wanted, so I never saw him again."

Sally had a girlfriend at college but said she was "told to get rid of her":

"Somebody told somebody, you know, so she didn't bother me again. I was upset; you would be."

Susie talked about loving the woman she was in a relationship with; she was finding it hard that the woman loved another girlfriend more. Sandra told us about her "special friend" with whom she had a non-sexual relationship: "When I see my friend, my eyes light up". It wasn't clear if Sandra wanted more from the relationship:

Interviewer: "Do you kiss her on the cheek?"

Sandra: "No, I dare not to."

Stephen also had a non-sexual relationship with his boyfriend. The couple had decided to take things slowly and get to know each other well before having sex with each other:

"I think we need to get to know each other, what each other likes, respect each other. And I believe that if you just go for sex straight away, if it's not what each other expects, it can just blow the whole thing out of the water really."

Sean's relationship with a man had been made difficult by the fact that his boyfriend was a wheelchair user. When they were out, people assumed that the relationship was based on Sean being a carer or personal assistant. Daffyd had a partner when the two of them were in a long-stay hospital, but they had not been able to keep in touch when he moved out.

Jim told us about a former relationship that had ended when the other man died. The two men had kept the relationship a secret from staff in the home where they lived. Sadly, this meant that when Jim's friend died, nobody took much care in telling him. He kept his grief a secret for several years:

Jim: "The supervisor just said he had a heart attack, just out of the blue like that. So, em, [long pause], so like em I felt, [pause], quite lonely, so like em, it's sort of like suddenly it's over because, [pause], bit of a shame."

Interviewer: "Did you think of him as your boyfriend? Is that how you thought of each other or something else?"

Jim: [long pause] "It's hard to say; eh, sort of like, close bondship. [pause] You know, stuff like that."

Sarah and Angelique had the most established relationship of the women that we met. They had been together for nearly four years. They spoke openly about how much they loved and supported each other, as well as the difficulties they faced with their families and with day-to-day tensions and arguments in the relationship. Sarah was asked what it was that she loved about Angelique so much:

> "Everything and everything – her body! I don't know, she protects me, she supports me, she listens to me, helps me out when I need help. She is with me 24/7. I was 23 [when they met]; Angelique was 19. She was a gorgeous one though. It was just that spark and seeing her for the first time and something just clicked in me. And I have proposed to her as well. She said, 'yeah' and it is just the money, trying to get money and then go and have the lesbian wedding and stuff like that."

Christine spoke about the day-to-day aspects of her relationship with a woman that she enjoyed – staying in, going to the cinema, getting take-aways:

> "What's being in love? Caring for somebody, it's just like loving somebody and being with them."

Owen said that having a boyfriend had made a big difference to his life as he had someone to share his difficult past with and spend time with:

> "I'd marry him tomorrow if I had the chance!"

Three of the men we spoke to told us about feelings for, and relationships with, male members of staff. Owen had in the past experienced strong feelings for a carer. He had found it difficult to cope with his feelings of attraction: "I would stand there crying." He told the member of staff that he fancied him and said that as a result he was asked to leave, because staff said that they didn't like it that he was gay.

Daffyd said that he had known several gay members of staff. He said that while they "hadn't tried anything on" with him, he would not have told anyone if they had. It seemed to us that Daffyd did not have a sense that it would be inappropriate for a member of staff to initiate something physical with him. Stefan did have a brief relationship with

his support worker, which ended when Stefan's mother found out and reported it:

> "One night he watched me singing at this karaoke thing ... he came in, watched me singing and he just said, 'I've got something to tell you, I'm gay'. Then we kiss and cuddled and saw each other for a little while. It's a shame because it's like, he's crossed the barrier there, he's meant to be there to support me, not the other ... I needed to go and tell his boss he was seeing me because my mum's a support worker. She knows the rules and the regulations and that they act on seeing clients and whatever."

Sex

The views and experiences of the people we met were as varied as those of any group of people would be. There were differences along gender lines – the women who had had sex with women had often also had sex with men and would compare the experiences:

> "But now when I go with a woman I find it's more pleasurable than with a bloke." (Angelique)

Whereas only one of the men talked about having sex with a woman:

> "Oh I have had sex with a woman when I was pesty [Welsh expression for 'horny'] enough and when you're drunk and any bugger comes back sort of thing, you know. Yeah, I have had sex with women." (Daffyd)

Only four of the women we talked to had had sex with another woman, and generally they had enjoyed the experience:

> "I had sex with a woman at the age of 20 and it was like whoa. What a hard thing to explain. I mean it was a good experience. It was." (Sarah)

Some of the women, like Christine, were reticent about discussing the sex they enjoyed, or what attracted them to women:

> Interviewer: "You have a good sex life with [girlfriend] then?"

Christine: "Oh yes."

Interviewer: "What is it you like about her, what is it about [girlfriend] that just turns you on?"

Christine: "Hum, that's a difficult question."

Interviewer: "You smile!"

Those women who had not had sex with another woman had obviously thought about it. Ann:

"I do want to be with another woman, and I do want to have sex with another woman. This is like a cancer eating away and I do want to be with another woman, and I do want to have sex with another woman ... but I'm never going to have that. I'm 42 and never had sex and never will."

The men generally had had more experience of sex with other men, and particular views on what they wanted. Sean said:

"But I would like it to be a two way thing. I've not had experience of you know – penetrative – touching and all that yeah – I've read about it. It would be a nice feeling to have that – that I could pleasure him and he could pleasure me."

A few of the men sometimes met men in toilets (cottaging) or known public parks (cruising) for sex. Jim said he enjoyed doing this:

"I'm just randomly going from one man to another. Safe sex mind. Never go without a condom."

Some of the men didn't like this idea and wanted to take things slowly. Stephen said:

"I believe kissing, cuddling somebody, caressing somebody is sex. It doesn't have to be the full sexual act. I'm a big believer in just having a cuddle, having a kiss. I don't believe in having one night stands. I don't do that. I really don't believe that. If I'm going to have sex with someone, yeah, I need time to get used to that person and to be respected by that person."

Jim recalled a very positive memory of having sex and spoke about the chance to embrace in the arms of a man he had just had sex with:

"I was still naked and it was so warm; just so nice. You can let all your worries go out of the window, you know – just total bliss."

Four of the men talked about using condoms, and the risks of contracting sexually transmitted infections (STIs). In Daffyd's case, the need for condoms had been only partly explained or understood. In the course of the interview he said that he did not have sex with anyone. But later he complained of getting headaches when he used condoms:

Interviewer: "What are you doing with the condom?"

Daffyd: "Oh, I just put it on."

Interviewer: "And then what?"

Daffyd: "I bin it then."

Interviewer: "So just masturbating."

Daffyd: "Yeah ..."

Interviewer: "So if you're just like masturbating by yourself, you don't need to use a condom."

Daffyd: "You don't?"

Interviewer: "No, only if there's someone else, so if it's just you just at home and you're masturbating, you don't need to use a condom, I mean you can if you want but you don't need to at all."

Daffyd: "Oh right, OK, thanks for telling me."

Only one of the women talked about STIs. Sally:

"... because you can get sexually transmitted diseases, that happens with either men or women."

What did people want from relationships?

Relationships were important to everyone and people routinely had clear ideas on what they wanted from them:

"Well I want someone to love and care for and I want to care for them as well. It works two ways. You can't give all the loving. They've got to give it back, haven't they?" (Pauline)

"It'd be company for you, you know, I've been alone all my life ... and I would live with him for ever then. We might fall out, but everyone falls out over something you know." (Daffyd)

Christine was clear she wanted her own space in any relationship:

"If you are still in love with somebody, you don't have to live with them, do you? Sometimes, I think, if you live together, then you start arguing; it's better to just have your own place."

Both men and women identified a number of barriers to finding, and having, relationships. One issue was a lack of privacy: nowhere to go without staff or neighbours knowing. Stephen, in common with several other people, only had a single bed in his bedroom:

"You've got to sleep on the floor if somebody does come. It's not the same then you know, and no privacy type of thing."

People said they lacked the confidence to speak to people they fancied and to go to places where they might meet other gay men or lesbians. Pauline:

"I don't know anything about where you go."

Other impairments, such as visual impairments and epilepsy, were also talked about as additional barriers. Having a learning difficulty was itself seen to be another obstacle. Ann said:

"I always feel you are kind of ... there is something inside that brain that kind of switches off. It's like, 'Don't talk to her, she's a disease....' I just feel they kind of, they talk to you as if you are a child. You should be seen and not heard."

Sean's view was that a non-disabled man would not want to have a relationship with him:

"We're always told to stick to your own kind – never have a relationship with non-disabled people, cos people say you're exploited."

What did people want from staff and services?

Everyone that we met had encountered at least one professional who had been immensely supportive in a range of different ways. The men and women in the study valued staff who were open, non-judgemental and who made time to talk to them about things that mattered. Sean highlighted the difference it had made for him to get support from an advocate:

"He makes me feel as if we're important, valued, as if we have an opinion, not just told to shut up."

Sarah and Angelique talked about the workers at their advocacy project, who had been a source of help and support: listening to them, finding out information for them and going to gay venues with them:

"They know we are gay. They just take us for how we are. They are not like, 'Oh my god here is the lesbians! Keep away!' They don't do that. They just take us for who we are. They are very nice." (Angelique)

Staff who did not shy away from talking openly about sex and relationships were valued. Ben communicated with a mixture of words and gestures. He had found it particularly useful when a professional used videos and visual images to explore the questions that he had about men having sex together. Ann said she had talked to her support worker about "adult things", including sex, and felt like an adult for the first time in her life.

Stephen was supported by a professional who was himself gay. The worker had taken him to a range of gay pubs in a big city so that he could decide what kinds of gay pubs he liked. Owen lived in a very rural location. He was supported in a similar way by a heterosexual member of staff to visit a gay pub. Daffyd was helped by staff in his home to fill in order forms for gay DVDs.

Support came from professionals from a wide range of backgrounds. Two men who lived in the same region had both had thoughtful responses from their psychiatrists. Paul's psychiatrist had put him in touch with a support group for gay, lesbian and bisexual people with learning difficulties, While Mark's psychiatrist had told him that it was important for him to meet other gay people and to develop relationships, including sexual relationships:

> "She thinks it's important to be yourself in that way. She says it's no use just living day to day, knowing what you are, if you can't express it."

There was a lot of gratitude expressed for support of this nature and quality. Ann talked about a professional in whom she had confided:

> "I just don't know what I would do without him. He has been a tower of strength. I just don't know how to thank him, you know what I mean."

Four people talked about the fact that a particular service they used felt "safe" as a whole: the service had a culture of acceptance that had made them feel OK to come out and they could be themselves there. In one service, staff had displayed pictures on the wall showing same-sex couples. Paul said that he really liked the pictures:

> Interviewer: "You like the pictures that are on the wall. What do they make you think about when you see those pictures?"
>
> Paul: "That it's alright to have anybody you love."

Unfortunately people were more likely to have experienced more negative than positive responses from staff and services. This had normally taken the form of outright homophobia or subtler forms of prejudice, which made people feel that it was not OK to be themselves. Stephen summed up a commonly held view that many staff frowned on same-sex relationships:

> "... people in services having a relationship, a lot of people can't take on board, having a gay relationship, it just doesn't happen. You're known to have a difficulty, you have a learning difficulty, OK you might

have a normal relationship, but it's a long way to a gay relationship. It just doesn't happen."

Owen told us that he had been asked to leave his group home when they found out he was gay: "They just said, 'I'm sorry we don't want you here; we don't like gay people.'" Sarah and Angelique had attended a youth club for people with learning difficulties but were repeatedly "told off" if they displayed any physical affection for each other. In common with other interviewees they highlighted the fact that while services seemed to have a lot of rules about not being sexist or racist, this did not seem to extend to not being prejudiced against gay, lesbian or bisexual users of the service:

> "On the youth club list, it says all the things that you should not do. No drugs, no smoking, no prejudice, no racism, take people as they are and I thought, 'Whooah, all that is shit. You don't take people for who they are. You are prejudice, because you have done it to me and my partner and I quit.'"

People seemed particularly critical of day services where few people had felt comfortable about being out:

> "I know a lot of people who are gay or lesbian who actually go to day centres, but they can't even discuss their sexuality, it's like, 'We won't have that kind of talk here'."

Several people told us about not being allowed to do things where they lived, like have other gay, lesbian or bisexual friends over, visit gay bars or wear certain clothes at home. Owen wanted to wear ripped jeans, as he had seen other gay men on the TV wearing them, but said that he couldn't:

> "It's not allowed here see, it's private, they're very strict here you know."

We asked our interviewees what practical support, if any, they wanted from staff and services. Three people were fluent about the fact that they wanted to support themselves and others more, rather than relying on staff and services. Two of these people had set up a support group for gay, lesbian and bisexual people with learning difficulties. The third wanted to establish a national advocacy project:

"How I see it being, like, is people who are gay and lesbian with learning difficulties coming into a really nice environment, talking about their own issues, supporting each other to get over issues they might be having difficulty getting over – some might be having real difficulty in wanting to tell their parents, but can't find how to tell them. Like a support group, but not the support role, more a friendship role, more a 'OK, let's go out for a drink', 'OK, let's book a room and have a meeting and talk about being gay or lesbian'." (Stephen)

People felt strongly that staff should see it as a part of their work to support people around their hopes and needs for same-sex relationships. Pauline had received some time-limited support from her psychologist. When the sessions finished, Pauline felt isolated and unsupported. She had wanted support to go to a pub where she might meet other lesbian women, but her psychologist had felt unable to provide this:

"She said, 'You're going to have to go to the pub and I can't take you to the pub'. She's not allowed to mix with us outside."

Staff opting out, or expressing concern, were seen as a making it harder to be open:

"Services – my opinion is that they're employed to support people, not discourage them, cos in the end you're gonna get people who think their sexuality is wrong." (Sean)

"It's actually taken me quite a while for people [in services] to understand I am who I am and let's get on with it. It's alright in my life, it's me that's dealing with the issues and all you do is support me with my issues. And that's been hard work. Just say it. If you're not happy with who I am, just say it. I'm not going to change who I am to please you. Tough luck! Get on and like me for who I am, or go and find a different job." (Stephen)

Both men and women wanted information on the emotional aspects of relationships. They wanted to know more about other gay, lesbian and bisexual people. As interviewers we were asked a lot of questions like, "What do other gay/lesbian people look like? What clothes do they wear? What jobs do they have? Where do they go out? What hobbies do they have?" Most people wanted to be supported to access pubs or clubs, but not everyone liked pubs and some people were more interested in going to groups where people talked or did not drink alcohol.

A clear model emerged of the kind of support that people wanted. Several people used the word "mentor" or "befriend" to describe their ideal kind of support – a member of staff who would actually go with them to gay and lesbian places and help them deal with their nerves or anxiety as well as transport. People described how they would like that person to be sensitive and tuned in to how they were feeling about being in a gay place and to be more present at some times and stand back a bit at others. Mark said he rarely went to gay pubs:

"You would need support, to support me in the environment, to make sure that nothing bad would happen to you. You couldn't just go by yourself. Even if I had just a friend to go with, I wouldn't be happy going with just them. I would want a figure around, or a mentor figure, who could support me, who could really help you, and make sure that you're OK. Somebody who would be in the background, so if something did happen, they could step in and help you and, just you know, help with the actual situation."

There were mixed views on whether people wanted the staff member to be gay, lesbian or bisexual themselves. Ben wanted to be supported by a gay member of staff, partly because he hadn't been happy when his heterosexual link worker had gone to a gay bar with him:

Interviewer: "Your link worker, is he gay?"

Ben: "No."

Interviewer: "No. So did he feel OK being in the bar with you?"

Ben: "No."

Interviewer: "And were you happy for him to go ..."

Ben: "No."

Overall, people wanted services to be more open – a word that was used time and time again. Sean encapsulated what many people told us – they wanted support to get a better kind of life:

"People say we're stupid and don't know anything. People don't understand – like in the day service – that we wanted a life."

Hopes and dreams for the future

We asked everyone about their hopes and dreams for the future. They talked among other things about becoming a parent and being in a relationship.

Being a parent

Five of the people in the study said they wanted to have children, including one man. Sally wanted children. Her family had asked her to wait and think about it, but she wasn't sure if she wanted to wait any longer. She had talked to a close gay male friend with learning difficulties about co-parenting. However, at the time of the interview she was actually being given injections to inhibit conception:

"Putting me straight away on the depot injection. Well they just said it was for my own good. My mum didn't want me to have a baby and neither do they, so? I suppose I can understand it but I should have a choice at the end of the day, you know. She just said yesterday that it is about money and everything, you know, space and that, and bringing the baby up and what have you. I knew all that already. I'm not stupid. They keep on asking me to wait, but I don't know if I want to."

Sally's gay male friend told us that staff in services had been trying to dissuade them from having a baby:

"We've been told by the services that it's a bad idea ... we've been put off. I don't think sexuality comes into it if you're good parents. I'd like to have a child and it's nice that she trusts me that way – to be a father. A child would be something to look forward to."

Pauline had given a considerable amount of thought to having a baby with another woman, though she was not in a relationship at the time of

the interview. Pauline had epilepsy and thought that her partner would have to be the one that had the child. Alternatively, she had thought that they could adopt though she was not sure if lesbians were allowed to adopt or not. Pauline worked with children and spoke at length about how much she loved babies:

"I'd like a baby, yes. I'd love a baby. Yeah, I do want a baby. I love babies. When I see babies in the shop I start talking to them and holding their little hands. I just like cuddling them and loving them and buying them nice clothes."

Angelique wanted to have a baby and had made an appointment with her GP to discuss IVF (in vitro fertilisation). Her partner, Sarah, was not sure about this, but accepted how much Angelique wanted to have a child and saw it as a natural part of their development as a couple and a family unit:

"I thought that, 'Well you want this baby, but I can't give you it babes'. It does break my heart a lot, it really does. Believe me, if I had any chance, any chance, I would do anything for her. She has, like, this fascination of having a baby and it is just like a story for me and her. We are working out when you get married and then right at the end you have a family and that is the end."

Being in a relationship

Most of the people we met were very clear that their dream for the future was to be in a relationship:

"I would like to live with him till one of us pops our clogs – that sort of thing." (Sean)

"I suppose my ultimate dream is to be with someone who I'm going to be with for the rest of my life, who I'm going to love and cherish for the rest of my life." (Stephen)

Ben, on the other hand, just wanted to meet more gay people and go to gay venues, while Jim wanted to have holidays at places where there were other gay men. He also wanted to live independently so that he could go out cruising whenever he liked. Robert was pessimistic about his future and his chances of finding a partner:

Interviewer: "And you were saying about how it would be nice to meet a partner or a boyfriend and I just wondered if you had like a picture of what that kind of future would be like?"

Robert: "... don't have a future ...."

Interviewer: "So you don't feel that's going to happen?"

Robert: "No."

Interviewer: "Do you feel alright about that or not?"

Robert: "No, no."

Interviewer: "Do you think that's something that you mind?"

Robert: "Mm-mm."

Interviewer: "You know you said that you're not sure that you will meet this lovely guy, or someone that you can be with, do you mind that you might not meet someone?"

Robert: "Mm-mm."

Interviewer: "That you might be single. Does that bother you?"

Robert: "Aye. It does."

Summary

- *Meeting other gay, lesbian and bisexual people* – There was a fairly even split between people who knew quite a few other gay, lesbian and bisexual people, and people who knew very few, if any. Overall, men were more likely than women to have social networks that included other gay people. The desire to meet and get to know other people was one of the strongest messages conveyed in our interviews. Most people had been to gay bars or clubs. Some had enjoyed this, but others had felt excluded or discriminated against on the scene or simply did not enjoy it.

- *Relationships* – Only a small number of people were in sexual/intimate relationships at the time of our interview although most had had experience of being in a relationship at some point in their lives. We heard accounts of all the positive and difficult things about being in relationships. One of the most positive features was having someone to do day-to-day things with.

- *Sex* – About half of the women we met had had sex with another woman and most talked about having had sex with men as well at some point in their lives. The men we met talked at greater length about the kind of sex they had, wanted and enjoyed with other men. Just under half of the men who were sexually active talked about issues to do with risk, safer sex and HIV.

- *What support do people want?* – People wanted staff to be supportive and non-judgemental about their sexuality. We heard some accounts of individual professionals, and some services, doing very positive and person-centred work with people to develop their sexuality or to lead sexual lives. However we also heard many instances of staff and services that had been unsupportive or hostile. In practical terms, people wanted tangible support from staff to meet other gay, lesbian and bisexual people and wanted staff to see this as a legitimate part of their job.

- *Hopes and dreams* – Five of the people in the study wanted to have children at some point in the future, although four of them said that they were being quite heavily dissuaded from this by staff and family members. Almost everyone else spoke about their hopes for the future in terms of being in a relationship.

4

How do staff and services approach work on relationships, sex and sexuality?

Jim's story

"Jim was just a quiet bloke, very nice, and we knew he was really interested in computers and technology and things, and he was often in the office and helping us install software on the computers. But other than that we didn't know very much about his life, really, or what he was interested in.

"I had a meeting with Terrence Higgins Trust (THT) and Paul [a gay member of staff at THT] said one of the things that he thought was really important when he was young, was seeing images that showed that it was OK to have same-sex relationships. And just anything tiny, small, it doesn't matter, someone in that situation will notice that and it will make them feel more welcome and it will make them just feel that they're OK. That one small step we could take as an organisation was just to have some images around the place and posters that would show that that was OK. So I asked him to send me some stuff that THT had, and so he did. And one of them was this postcard that said, 'Pride not prejudice' and it had a picture of two men on it. And Jim kept looking at this, he kept taking it off the pin board and looking at it, but I still didn't...

"Anyway he kept looking at this postcard, and I still didn't really think anything of it. And then things with THT were progressing and we were talking about doing a kind of road show to all the day services. So we were designing this poster and it said something like, you know, 'Some men fancy women, some men fancy men and women, and some men just fancy other men'. And Paul faxed it through to me with the draft of this poster, and Jim was there when the fax came through cos he was always in the office and

that's when he said, 'That's what I fancy ... men', he said, 'This is me'.

"So then he came out to the whole staff team. And it just happened that Jim was out. Suddenly it was like everybody knew that Jim was a man who fancied men.

"I mean, he might be someone that you could interview when you come back and interview people who have learning difficulties, and he can then tell you a lot about his experiences, but they are pretty harrowing experiences within day services. I mean, one of the things was about ... and this is just awful, I'm sure it happens to other people as well, not necessarily who've got learning difficulties – but he'd had a close relationship with this guy in a day service who then died. And he just didn't turn up one day so Jim had to ask where he was and then he was told he was dead ... mm, this is quite upsetting to talk about [pause] ... sorry....

"So of course because the relationship wasn't open, no-one would tell Jim that this man had died. So he had to ask and then be told in quite ... so to be told that was just obviously devastating. And of course then he couldn't be open about his grief [interviewee upset], you know, none of the closeness of the relationship, or the relationship at all was known about, and so none of the consequences of that being, you know, well not just over but for this person who had died, was appreciated by anybody that was there. And Jim just had to, you know, carry all of that himself; he couldn't tell anybody about it. He didn't tell anybody until he told us. [interviewee crying]

"And it was years ago. It happened years ago. You know, that is something that he carried around for years and didn't tell. And of course when he did tell, we were crying, he was crying and you know that suffering really is a consequence of it not being OK for him to be gay in a day service. You can't have rules about people not having sexuality, because they have it anyway." (Manager in advocacy service)

The next two chapters draw on our interviews with 71 staff in 20 learning difficulty services across the UK. We wanted to know how, or if, staff and services were supporting men and women with learning difficulties to think about their relationships, including intimate and sexual relationships. Our assumption was that services that were already addressing these issues might be more likely to be open to including discussion and reflection on being gay, lesbian or bisexual. This chapter discusses how services related to sex and sexuality in general and the opportunities for, and obstacles to, doing work in this area that staff described.

Our interviews with staff began by asking what work on sex, sexuality and relationships was going on; were there courses and groups available, for example? Did intimate relationships and sexuality feature in person-centred planning?

Approaches to work on sex, sexuality and relationships

A common response of services was to offer work or groups on relationships and sexuality only if service users explicitly said that this was something they wanted. It was suggested that the issue should 'come from people themselves' rather than be put forward by staff. Here, two support workers talk about a woman who used the day service where they worked:

Staff 1: "This lady hasn't got a partner."

Staff 2: "And it's desperately what she wants."

Staff 1: "She's looking for anybody, because she needs somebody. So anybody would do, to a degree, I think. She latches on to ladies too, as well as gentlemen. So

we don't know about her sexuality. I don't think she knows. I don't think she has any concept. I would imagine she thinks she would have to have a boyfriend because we all have."

Interviewer: "Would you or other staff members ever proactively raise or discuss whether people wanted to express themselves sexually in a relationship?"

Staff 2: "I don't think I would raise it. I wouldn't presume myself to think what I thought they wanted out of a relationship unless there was some hint that they'd said to me first. I wouldn't go to somebody and say ..."

Staff 1: "Do you want?"

Staff 2: "I'd feel quite intrusive doing that."

Staff 1: "This lady would just so much enjoy a relationship, I think. I mean, from your research and things, are you sort of saying, right, OK, then we should be speaking to her and saying, 'Is this what you want'? At home they've sort of treated it, 'Oh right, well, we'll say there are other nice things in life, so you can have a nice warm, you know, aromatherapy bath and things'. And in a way that's not what she's wanting, and I think she is saying, 'I need to be sexually active'. You know, and how do we go about it, because of the home situation ... she lives in a group home. But maybe we should. Maybe we should be thinking about it from her point of view."

Staff 2: "We did a lot of work quite a few years ago about how far you should go and what are your responsibilities, how far you feel comfortable.... And I think we generally thought at the time that it was all a bit in your face ... um but I don't know."

Staff 1: "I would feel that if somebody likes this lady ... whatever ... even if it was same-sex ... we should give the same support. Maybe we've got to show them that they have a choice. Unless we give them the opportunity to choose then they're never going to choose, are they really? I mean, I think what we're saying is we think a lot of the people here are asexual. We're kind of thinking that it doesn't happen here."

Staff 2: "Yeah. But actually unless somebody actually comes up to you and asks for your help or anything? I haven't really picked up on a great deal."

Staff 1: "And actually they probably won't unless we give them the opportunity, really. And even the opportunity to think initially that this is OK. I think it's something we've got to talk about as a team."

When we explored the idea of letting the issue come from service users in our interviews, it seemed that a number of different things were going on which we look at in more detail later in this chapter:

- a belief that it was intrusive, and inappropriate, to bring up issues around relationships and sexuality, unless it came from a person with learning difficulties themselves;
- fear of doing work in this area, because of a lack of policy or guidance or a lack of confidence, experience or opportunities for training;
- concerns about the reactions of others, usually parents and/or carers.

Taking the lead from women and men with learning difficulties?

In our interviews with staff in day services, we were told that the content of courses and groups was rarely pre-determined but set by service users' own concerns and ideas:

"When the need arises we run a relationships group. The way we see them working is that people talk about issues that are important to them. If you pre-agenda it you might actually ... you might end up talking about things that aren't necessarily that important and railroading people." (Support worker in day service)

Several staff, in different services, commented on the perceived inappropriateness of looking as if they were pushing their own agenda. A manager of services in the independent sector reflected on his years of experience and explained why he thought it was right to take a lead from service users:

"Without wanting to seem to be either complacent, or not responsive, we do tend to take our lead from the individual. We're not about having rules that everybody by age so and so will have had these

experiences. Some of us have been around long enough to have gone from the time when nothing was mentioned, through the time when anything and everything was possible. And not just possible but desirable, and possibly even more than desirable – required."

If the topic of relationships or sexuality had not been identified by service users, then some staff recognised that the issue was ignored – or at least ignored until there was a 'crisis'. So, for example, most of the day centres that took part in this study reported problems in responding to men who had sex with other men on the premises. Commenting on this, a staff member in another setting told us:

"The local day centre found a couple having sex in the shed and guess what the day centre did to deal with the problem? They took down the shed. I think that says it all, doesn't it?"

A few interviewees challenged the idea that staff should wait for issues to do with relationships and sexuality to come from men and women with learning difficulties themselves before discussing the subject. Staff working in a large independent residential services organisation recognised that work often needed to be proactive, to ensure that people had the information that they needed. Here, people's needs for support around sexuality and relationships were part of the review for individuals' planning meetings, to ensure that they did not get lost or ignored. A lecturer in a further education (FE) college, when told that a dominant theme in our interviews was staff saying that it was not right for them to bring up sexuality, commented:

"Oh right. The thing is I really disagree, because you can't bring up something that you don't know exists or you don't know is OK to bring up."

A health promotion worker we spoke to was looking at adapting a young people's community-based sex education course for people with learning difficulties. This was to culminate in a residential weekend for the group, and the building of a web page. She had not previously worked with services for people with learning difficulties and saw sex education as an obvious right for all young people – disabled and non-disabled – whatever their sexuality.

In one advocacy service we visited, funds for a campaigns worker had been secured; it had been proposed that sexuality would be one of the first campaigns. This service saw social and leisure activities outside of the day centre as a way that people might choose whom they wanted to spend their leisure time with. The service saw it as part of their role to support people to feel less isolated, to have more friends and to support people who wanted to have girlfriends or boyfriends:

> "But we're thinking of trying to do something more explicit, because one of the things members told us was that they wanted a dating agency. Because people wanted to meet people." (Support worker)

A lecturer in an FE college spoke of her work around self advocacy where relationships and friendships were routinely discussed by students. However sexuality and sexual relationships did not form part of the 'official curriculum':

> "But I feel obliged to widen it. I don't feel I could teach fairly to students for a year and not bring in themes like sexuality. You know you spend hours talking abut the rights to money and the rights to Giro, the rights to a safe working environment, when actually very few of our students collect their money, or really have an awareness of their money, or are going to go into paid work. But 90% of my students will at some point have a relationship."

Barriers for staff in doing work around sexuality and relationships

The majority of staff in our interviews expressed concern about their ability to work with people with learning difficulties in the area of sexuality and relationships. Many of them indicated a frustration that they did not engage with these issues, but felt constrained from doing so for a number of reasons. In services that did not have policy statements on how staff should work in this area, staff felt unconfident, and unwilling, to do the work. They were concerned about things going wrong and there not being a policy available to

back up their work. The absence of training in this area also left staff feeling underskilled and unsure.

Confidence, willingness, experience

A lack of confidence or experience meant several staff said that they chose to ignore the needs of the people they supported. Several of our interviewees in one service were young support workers in small residential homes. Pressed on how they would support someone who wanted to develop a sexual relationship, one said:

> "It would be quite hard if he says, 'I want this'. Sounds horrible but I don't think I'd want to, you know. I'd just get the unit manager involved and if something did go completely wrong it's on his shoulders isn't it?"

Many of the staff interviewed said that they thought that some of their service users were "confused" about their sexuality, which made it difficult to know how to support them. Staff, in turn, were themselves unsure and confused. A deputy manager of a day service, for example, commented:

> "We've two people whom, I'm not sure what their sexuality is, not that it's any of my business what their sexuality is, but I wouldn't like to say that I knew what their preference is. I think they're very, very confused, but that's not really the right word, 'unsure' of what they feel. So as I say, I think we really tend to bury our heads in the sand and think, 'We'll let it go'."

A group worker in another day service talked about his uncertainty about the relationships between people's sexual behaviour and their sexual identity:

> "There doesn't seem to be a clear indicator that you know they're heterosexual or homosexual.... They seem to sort of swing between the two.... There are people who are having homosexual relationships, but they also have a girlfriend.... They seem to think that it's important to be seen as having a girlfriend or a boyfriend. Which is quite odd."

A common view expressed in our interviews was that the sexual contact that men and women with learning difficulties initiated, or experienced, was not related to sexual identity, but was an expression of sexual need in an environment that offered limited choices. As a result, services often asked themselves first, and sometimes, solely, if the relationship was abusive or exploitative. Staff sometimes thought men who had sex with men were not necessarily gay, but only had men to choose from. Some women who had sex, or physical intimacy, with other women also had boyfriends. Staff tended not to interpret this as indicating that these women had a lesbian or bisexual identity. As a result, they did not feel the need to discuss sexual identity, but focused instead on behaviour, if it became problematic.

By contrast, a minority of services had staff who were trained, experienced and confident in this area. In a service that routinely included sexuality and relationships in reviews, staff said that detailed record keeping of discussions and decisions made them feel safe and supported:

"As long as we're clear and we've thought about what we're doing and why, and it's written down somewhere, so the teams are not just going off and doing their own thing; if we've considered what we're doing, then we should be OK."

A member of staff in another service also demonstrated confidence in this area, working with people in a way that did not make any assumptions about sexual identity, but aimed to help each individual to discover their feelings:

"I was working with a man yesterday. I was just doing some assessment work and I was showing him drawings of sexual relationships and I said, 'Would you like to do this?' It was two men kissing, and I said, 'What are they doing?' and he said, 'They are snogging', and I said, 'Would you like to snog someone?' and he said, 'Yeah.' When I got the other picture which was male and female and I said, 'This is two men and this is a man and a woman. You said that you would like to snog someone, which would you prefer? Would you prefer this one or this one?' He said, 'Oh the woman, I would like to snog the woman', and I said, 'If two men want to snog each other, do you think that is alright?' and he said, 'Yeah, yeah that is alright.' And I said, 'Is it what you would like to do, because', I said, 'I think it is alright as well'. He said, 'No, no, I would like to snog a woman'. Which kind of made me fairly confident that he was showing a

heterosexual preference. It wasn't based on prejudice, it wasn't based on his own attitude, he wasn't disgusted, he was yeah, fine ... that is what I like."

Staff commented on the lack of helpful and accessible resources around same-sex relationships (hence the resources subsequently developed as part of this project, see the Appendix). Communication systems often did not include anything on sex, let alone on same-sex relationships.

Policies

It was quite common for staff not to know if their service or organisation had a policy about work on sex and sexuality. They routinely said they had an equal opportunities policy but this was unlikely to say very much – if anything – about how staff should work in the area of sex and sexuality. One manager in a service that staff had claimed did not have any relevant policies observed:

"Whilst people have constantly been moaning, 'We have got no guidelines, we have got no strict protocols or criteria or frameworks within which to do this work', that is not actually correct. I actually found quite a lot of materials around and you know, dust gathered – and that is not bemoaning the domestic services here, it is because they are rarely taken off the shelves because they remain as a sensitive issue."

The majority of staff interviewed said they needed and wanted policies. Two of the services visited in the study were in an authority that *was* drafting a sex and sexuality policy for *all* its learning disability services. One independent provider had just written a draft policy, which included an upfront statement about the value of same-sex relationships and encouraged staff to be proactive in terms of offering support to all service users in the area of personal and sexual relationships. An area service manager elsewhere described how a new policy had come about because of reactions to various 'crises' relating to sex in day centres. Staff in different centres had been reacting differently to service users having sex on the premises and there were no clear guidelines setting out how they should respond. A new draft policy had been widely consulted upon.

33

Policies were regarded as helpful if, and when, they gave work in the area legitimacy, especially in the face of criticism. One support worker we interviewed felt that the organisation's policy on personal relationships enabled her to be assertive with parents. In one case in which she was involved parents were very opposed to their son's same-sex relationship and had involved a local priest in trying to get the service to *not* support it. However, the service had a policy around supporting sexual relationships including same-sex relationships:

> "They've got their own opinion but these are our policies and we can't change them. We showed them the policy and said, 'This is how we're going to work it ... they're both consenting and we can't stop it'."

A senior manager in another service, which had historically had a lot of parental involvement, said:

> "I think it's fairly challenging to families. Originally it was very much the policy that the families had to be made aware that this was in fact the policy. And I don't know whether it was because it was fairly challenging in traditional terms ... I mean for instance, it supports the idea that people can have same-sex relationships."

Policies could also serve to challenge staff who were ambivalent or negative about same-sex relationships. For example, one manager in an independent residential service told us that their policy was very clear that:

> "Part of the organisation's expectations of you is that you may have your own personal and ethical/moral beliefs, but on occasion we might ask you to set those aside in order to provide an appropriate support for someone we're working with, and that might be challenging for you."

This organisation provided services for a range of people, including individuals living independently and those with profound and multiple impairments. Regardless of whom they were working with, staff were expected to include sexuality in each person's plan:

> "What we've said to people is that somewhere in their individual plan, there has to be a reference to need or potential needs around sexuality. And even if you don't know what that is, or this person maybe isn't seemingly demonstrating that you need to ... you also need to acknowledge that. If you're not aware of any, then OK, but we need you to write something down because we want you to have at least considered it, rather than just saying, 'Oh no, this person doesn't.'" (Development worker in independent, residential service)

Where there were policies, issues relating to same-sex relationships were written about in quite different ways – some more positively than others. Some policies stressed that same-sex relationships should be treated as any other; some recognised that people would face discrimination; and some focused more on issues of risk and consent:

> "Yeah, same-sex rel- ... cos what does it say? It says that it's fine if there is understanding and consent. I mean there is a little section about lesbian ... I can't remember off hand what it says. But anyway, basically we can't stop it. It's their lives, they can do what they want." (Support worker in independent residential service)

One sex education worker we talked to thought that any policy needed to explicitly recognise that women might have same-sex relationships:

> "... because that seems to be a forgotten thing.... So instead of just having the gay label that's supposed to cover everything that actually people take as meaning men, make it more specific that it covers women, and some sort of issue around bisexuality there as well."

In services that positively supported same-sex relationships, policies, especially the equal opportunities policy, were seen as supporting a respectful culture. In these, same-sex relationships were explicitly stated to be equal to heterosexual relationships. Remarks that could be seen as sexist or homophobic would routinely be challenged, and complaints taken seriously.

In a service with a large workforce, senior managers wanted all staff to understand that the intention of their 'diversity policy' was to be effective. To emphasis this, they undertook a survey into people's experiences of discrimination in the workplace, which was repeated every two years to see if experiences were changing:

"We also provide training around diversity generally and around sexuality specifically, and I think again that sends out a strong message. And I think it's the cultural thing really, isn't it, and it's about me standing up in front of people and saying, 'I don't want to read, "this organisation is homophobic" when I do this survey in two years' time. And I've got some responsibility for that but so have all of you.' And then reinforcing that through producing policies, through the work we do. Through not being afraid when we're talking about diversity, to say diversity includes issues around sexuality. I think it's just kind of ... it's the dripping tap effect really, isn't it? Just keep saying it and people will get the message." (Chief executive in independent residential service)

Some staff elsewhere expressed concerns that it was difficult to write policies in the field of relationships, including intimate relationships. While some services wanted to have clear policies with detailed guidelines, others wanted looser guiding principles.

It became clear to us that there was often some difference of opinion between services managers and front line staff. A chief executive in a service that wanted to have an effective policy document commented:

"People want prescription because it makes them feel safe. And I know they get a bit frustrated with me when I say, 'But it's not possible to do that, because you can't write a policy that's going to cover every single possibility, permutation, eventuality'. So it has to be about setting the framework again, sending out the message, 'This is where we want you to go'. And if you're not sure in your particular service whether something should be happening or not, well then, discuss it. That's why we have the line management process. And if your line manager's not sure, they should discuss it. And ultimately, if people are unclear or uncertain or want to know that they're going to get backed, I suppose it would come to me and then I'd have to make a decision. And I would do that on the basis of the circumstance and the information I was given."

By contrast a support worker, voicing opinions we heard in several services, said:

"I think there seems to be a big grey area ... I certainly am not sure where I stand and what I'm supposed to be supporting people with and how to support people. It seems to be very grey. I'd like it to be black and white. I'd like to know what I'm supposed to be doing, how I can do that and you know, by the law, what I can and can't do."

One clear message from staff was that they were not prepared to make 'difficult' decisions about how to support people with learning difficulties in isolation from their managers or other colleagues, regardless of whether policies were in place:

"What I learnt on the sexuality training was that any decision, as long as you don't make it on your own, if it's something a bit tricky, if you sit down as a support worker and say, 'Well, so and so wants to go to gay bars', or whatever it is, if you sit down and discuss it with other managers, sort of note it down, you know no-one's going to prosecute you unless you've done something absolutely ludicrously unsafe."

One advocacy organisation felt that not only staff, but service users as well, needed to be familiar with policies, especially on equal opportunities:

"We've got an accessible version but we need to do two things – to promote what the policy says in pictures and photographs that are around the building so that people can see it, because I think that words aren't the greatest way of letting people know what something's about, and then provide some kind of training for everybody in the organisation about it."

Training

Most staff told us that a lack of training held them back from doing work around sex, sexuality and relationships. Training in these issues was not always prioritised:

"There's only a certain amount in the training budget and they'll pick out the training that definitely needs doing and move other stuff to one side." (Support worker in day service)

Most staff who had attended training had found it helpful and were positive about it. One lecturer in an FE college said that training around exploring sexuality for adults with learning difficulties had been challenging and had had a profound impact on her work. As a result, she felt committed to including relationships as part of the curriculum on advocacy and speaking up.

One area service manager highlighted training as the main way to change and challenge staff attitudes:

"There are people working in our services who shouldn't be there – they've got the wrong approach. It's hard to change that, but we can't back away from them, so we need to challenge values and attitudes."

A residential provider we visited also saw relationships and sexuality as a vitally important part of staff training. Four workshops a year were run in that service. A lot of work was done on people's values and beliefs, to bring out how these affected their work, especially around relationships and sexuality. It was emphasised in the training that staff were expected to set personal beliefs aside, if they conflicted with meeting a person's needs.

The fpa (formerly The Family Planning Association) was mentioned by several services as having provided very useful training in the area of sexuality. Often these courses had been used subsequently by services as templates for their own training.

Issues about same-sex relationships were normally one component of training around sexuality in general. One training officer was unsure if the right balance between different sexualities was struck:

"If you go straight in and talk about the lesbian issues and they don't have the basics about sexuality in general, are they going to be, 'What are you talking about?' But then if you do the whole of sexuality you tend to marginalise gay and lesbian relationships in the training."

Staff in one service had found the training around sex and sexuality that they had experienced too provocative and challenging. They felt that the approach taken by the trainer was unhelpful:

"We did have a lady who came and raised ... she was a bit like a devil's advocate lady – she came and threw all these ideas on to the table ... outraged everybody." The close link between training and policy was outlined by one service. During training, staff had asked what back up there was for them when working around sexuality issues:

"People would come on the training, raise awareness, all sorts of things would be disclosed and then they would say, 'But where's the back up for us in the workplace? You know, can we allow this? Should we stop that? What can we do about whatever?'"

The outcome in this service was that the training manager eventually decided not to embark on any major strategic training in the absence of a policy and, as there was no policy, no training was being offered to staff.

Concerns about the reactions of others

The possible adverse reactions of parents and carers were routinely cited as a source of anxiety for staff, which could sometimes get in the way of doing work around sex, sexuality and relationships. Most staff acknowledged that they took account of the views of parents and carers:

Staff: "I suppose there's a reliance on service users coming forward to staff and we're not making the step towards them to say, 'This is OK, you can talk about it'."

Interviewer: "Why do you think that is?"

Staff: "Um ... fear I think [laughter] of, you know, backlash from, you know, carers or residential staff."

An FE college manager we spoke to commented:

"We've had two different responses around the parent issue: one is either, 'Don't you dare make my son or daughter gay or talk with them about that stuff', and the other has been, 'Oh I do hope my son's gay, cos then he can't get anyone pregnant'."

One service found that they often needed to engage with parents if the person with learning difficulties lived at home. In one particular instance, they had been working with a gay man whose mother was described as quite homophobic. Over time, staff found that by listening to her concerns – and showing that they were listening – her views changed:

"She was scared of the risk and vulnerability and she didn't want him to be hurt or exploited in any way and her perception of other gay men was a dirty raincoat type image and the sort of predatory type situation. I think what started it was I explained to her that we come from the same place, that we want to protect him too, but we do that through education and through support and by getting his cooperation and trust. That we can have some positive input when he does go out and form relationships, rather than him going out on his own and trying to hide it from everyone. That argument, I think, convinced her that he was going to go out anyway and it was better that he was supported, rather than trying to be stopped." (Member of day centre staff)

Several services had explicit policy statements that made clear that their role was to support the service user in a number of different areas of their lives, including relationships. One service had funded, and supported, a gay man with learning difficulties to attend a conference in London about gay, lesbian and bisexual people with learning difficulties. The service knew that the man's mother would oppose this but decided that she did not need to know:

"We thought, 'Oh, we're sending him to London. We're paying for him to go. We're not going to be there. We're not supporting it. His mum doesn't even want him to go anywhere without thinking it's with us.' And I purposely didn't tell her what he was going to London for, and I just thought, if anything goes wrong, she's going to find out that he was going to go to this conference about being gay and having learning difficulties and it will be in London. But I just thought, 'Well, we'll do it anyway and probably nothing will go wrong', and nothing did go wrong. But, yeah, I mean, I just thought our project is for him, it's not for his mum. And I'd just have to take the flak as the manager really, wouldn't I?" (Community participation worker in advocacy service)

Four of the staff we interviewed talked about the disabling impact of Section 28 of the 1988 Local Government Act on doing work in this area (the act applied only in England, Wales and Scotland). Although this has now been repealed, it seemed that misunderstandings about Section 28 (which had prohibited the promotion of homosexuality by local authorities) might continue to impede work in this area for some time to come.

By contrast, the services that had done the most innovative work around sexuality and relationships indicated real confidence in their values and beliefs in taking the work on:

"We were a bit nervous as an organisation to tackle the topic. And then suddenly we said, 'No we're doing it' and actually … well it's fine. It was fine, it was just doing it that was the mental block."

Summary

- *Approaching work on sex and sexuality* – In most services, the issues of sex, sexuality and relationships were not introduced into groups, activities or plans unless service users actively brought them up. A small number of staff in a minority of services took a different approach and were proactive in raising these issues.
- *Barriers to doing the work* – In this area there were concerns – and some reticence – about doing work in this area. These related to a lack of experience and confidence, gaps in policy and training provision and concerns about the adverse reactions of other people.
- *Policies* – There were only a small number of services with detailed policies that included specific references to same-sex relationships. The majority of staff wanted clearer policies that gave detailed guidance on how to support men and women with learning difficulties in this area of their lives. However some managers were unsure about how to write detailed policy guidance that would cover every eventuality.
- *Training* – This was recognised as an important way of gaining expertise and challenging views and attitudes. Most staff had attended some training on personal relationships and were positive about it. However for many staff, the

training had been some time ago and had not routinely covered same-sex relationships.

• *Concerns about the reactions of other people* – Several staff said they felt inhibited from supporting people in this area of their lives, because they feared the adverse reactions of other significant people in the person's life – especially parents and carers. Some services had worked carefully, over a long period of time, to establish a good dialogue with parents in this area. Some services were trying to be more explicit about the service upholding the rights of the service user, which might or might not always sit comfortably with their families.

Professionals' experiences and views of same-sex relationships for people with learning difficulties

This chapter presents accounts from staff about their experiences of working with, supporting or knowing people with learning difficulties who were having, or who seemed to want to have, a same-sex relationship. Five of our 71 interviewees said that they had no experience of this, including a psychologist in a primary care trust who told us that the issue of same-sex relationships had never come up in his clinical practice. However, some of these staff did acknowledge that they might not be aware of people's relationships, even if they did exist. One day service manager, for example, said:

> "There's no known clients who have same-sex relationships. If there are any people who do, then they're very well-hidden. In the past there's been a horrible culture of people with learning difficulties assumed to be asexual. So I wouldn't say that there aren't people here who would like a same-sex relationship. They're just hidden."

In our interviews with staff who did have experience of people with learning difficulties who wanted to have a same-sex relationship several themes emerged. These themes form the basis of this chapter. They are:

- people with learning difficulties feeling ashamed about wanting to have a same-sex relationship;
- a lack of privacy and space to have a relationship;
- the hidden nature of women's relationships with women;

- staff attitudes to same-sex relationships;
- difficulties in accessing a gay, lesbian and bisexual 'scene' and culture;
- cross-dressing;
- opportunities for, and obstacles to, supporting and sustaining same-sex relationships;
- homophobia and heterosexism in learning disability services.

People with learning difficulties feeling ashamed about wanting to have a same-sex relationship

Staff told us repeatedly about the guilt and shame that people with learning difficulties felt about their feelings for people of the same-sex. A support worker in a day service, for example, described how one man she supported regarded his sexual behaviour and feelings as inherently bad:

> "He's sort of wrapped up in this sort of, 'Oh it's naughty, it's bad, you know I shouldn't be doing it'. I mean he's in his late 40s and his family don't know and he doesn't want to come out to his family. So there's all sorts of guilt around how he feels, you know, about his sexuality. Lots of confusion in that, you know, he really wants it but feels guilty about expressing it, or being open about it."

A lecturer in a further education (FE) college reported a similar experience in her work with one student, using images of couples depicted in hetero- and homosexual relationships:

"I work with a male student who presents in quite an effeminate way. Oh it's just little things that he has, like he always carries around a pink handbag that says 'Girl power' and he just talks.... He's very.... He just presents it in a way that my guess would be, you know, that he would like to perhaps explore a same-sex relationship.... I was just really interested to see how this student would start exploring things.

"And I sort of put the images out on the floor and the students sort of sat round looking at them, and this student walked straight up to this image that I have of two men kissing and he just said, 'That's disgusting, that's dirty.' And I was really shocked. I just hadn't expected that to come out.

"And I sort of said, 'Do you want to talk about that?', you know, 'Shall we talk about that?' And he said, 'Oh it's dirty', and I sort of said, 'Well what do you mean?' He said, 'Well, my mum's told me that that's dirty', and we sort of looked at what they were doing and they were kissing. That actually kissing's a very natural thing to do. You know a lot of us in the room said that, 'Yeah, we'd kissed people before, and actually it's not dirty. You know, it's actually very natural and very comfortable and clean.' And he just kept saying, 'Well my mum's told me that that's dirty'. So that was an example of a reaction.

"Then you know, when we looked at it further, he actually said, 'Oh actually, that's nice. It's nice, they look happy. But it's dirty. I'd like that, but it's dirty.' And it was so sad, because you just got the feeling that he may have tried to explore things in the past and, I mean, this is just my sort of perception, that it just felt like somebody had really said to him, 'Stop doing that, that's dirty.' It wasn't even his voice when he looked at this picture. It just sounded like he was using what his mum had said to him.

"And so I worked with that student over a sort of second year and now when we look at those images that doesn't come out any more, he just sort of tends to pick that image and look at it."

A lack of privacy and space to have relationships

Lack of private spaces for people to have physical intimacy in day services was presented as a major problem. When combined with uncertainty or ambivalence about how to respond to demonstrations of same-sex sexuality, it often led to relationships being ignored or hidden. A group worker in a day service, for example, said:

"There seemed to be a whole sort of gay men's group in the male toilets here. People knew about it, but nothing was really, you know, it was never really acknowledged. It was just something that happened. I mean, for that to be around and for them to have to use, you know, a toilet, you know, it's terrible that it went unacknowledged. There's just no private space for people to be together."

Partly because of the lack of space and opportunity for physical intimacy, men with learning difficulties were reported to frequently use public sex environments, especially toilets. This was true of one of the students of a teacher in a residential FE college who described what happened:

"And he got in with all the local fraternity here who are users at worst, some of these chaps. And one chap had obviously introduced him to pickups in toilets. But he didn't know when to stop. So of course, every time he was let out of the door he was up the local and, well, it doesn't take long in a place like this for the old biddies to see what's going on. He was given a good hiding up there once by somebody. We tried everything. We showed films, we talked to him, psychiatric service. Didn't make a scrap of difference. He was just off out the door and wallop."

Time and again we were told about men's experiences of sexual and physical assault, mostly as victims, but sometimes as offenders:

"There was a service user on this ward and he was obviously gay, but he was abusing all the men there. There was 17 on the ward at that time and he was forever found in the toilets with them all. And he was absolutely bullied, and it used to upset me, but it was a culture that was accepted because he was gay; it was acceptable to call him whatever, everything you

could think of. He was called it by the cook, the cleaners, everyone that'd step on to the ward. I felt it was only me that kind of thought, 'This poor guy here, yeah, he is gay but....' He was always laughed at."
(Service manager in long-stay hospital)

Lack of privacy also extended to concerns about the nature and extent of information that was recorded about people's behaviour. A member of staff in a day service commented on a file that had been sent from a residential home to the day service about a man with learning difficulties:

"It goes into real depth around how excited he was while watching TV where there were naked men or something. And you know, it's just outrageous the sort of language they were using ... and you know, he's just expressing his sexuality."

The hidden nature of women's relationships with women

Staff were clear that the issues around the sexuality of women with learning difficulties were quite different from men's. While men's same-sex identity, and their expressions of it, were often obvious and/or problematic, women interested in developing a relationship with other women were not easily noticeable or identified. An advocacy worker saw this as an extension of the lack of visibility of lesbians in society generally:

"One of the challenges here is about lesbians being, you know, invisible.... Lesbians in general are invisible and lesbians with learning disabilities even more invisible."

A support worker in a self advocacy organisation reflected on why a group set up for lesbian, gay and bisexual people with learning difficulties had attracted so few women:

"I think it's partly that women's sexuality generally not being recognised. A lot of the men, professionals have put them in touch with us, because to some extent they're seeing it as a problem. Whereas I think maybe with women, you know, it's not being identified as a problem because it's not being identified at all. I think it gets minimised to, 'Oh, that's just two women

friends', you know, it's never seen as it might possibly be a sexual relationship or develop into one."

A male worker, reflecting on the fact that he could not think of any lesbians with learning difficulties he had worked with, said:

"If you see two women cwtching [cuddling], you think, 'Oh look', but if you see two men cwtching, it's, 'Oh, what are they up to?'"

A college tutor we spoke to began to question the way she saw the relationship of two women she was working with, just before our research interview with her:

"They're just holding hands and they're walking back from the park. I just thought, 'They could really be in a relationship, those two'. And so I just looked at it from another way, maybe because I was having this interview here today. I was just thinking that it'd be really nice if they wanted to express that sexually, if they knew how to do that."

A teacher in an FE setting told us that her students with learning difficulties also assumed that women's relationships together would be platonic. She contrasted the responses of her students to a picture of two men kissing and then a picture of two women kissing:

"The image of the two men, most of the students go, 'Oh!' shocked, you know, 'That's dirty', or whatever, 'That's not natural.' Two women, they always say, 'Oh they're friends, they're good friends'. And I always say, 'Well, if you look at them they're actually kissing, and I don't kiss my friends on the mouth. I would say that they're in love. I would say that they're more than friends. They're actually girlfriend and girlfriend.' 'No, they're just really good friends.' It's so interesting. Not that it's dirty or awful, just that they just cannot.... It's almost not recognised. It's almost like, 'Well, women and women – that doesn't happen'. I've got an image of two women, one sat on another one's knee with their arms around them and even then, 'They're sisters', 'Mother and daughter' – really interesting."

One lesbian worker supported a woman with learning difficulties who she felt really wanted to have a relationship with another female service user. However, while this seemed clear to this member of staff, she felt that the relationship that was going on between the two women was largely hidden to other staff:

"Women can get away with a lot more, I think, in terms of, you know, sort of being friends and being really close friends and maybe being quite intimate but people really not acknowledging that they might be lesbian."

A number of staff commented that they could think of few resources aimed at women with learning difficulties, which included information about, or images of, lesbians.

Staff attitudes to same-sex relationships

As we have seen earlier, staff attitudes can determine the whole way that the relationships of many people with learning difficulties they work with are considered; for example, that same-sex relationships are automatically viewed as problematic:

"I mean, the first thing that comes into my head when that [same-sex relationship] comes up is that it is normally a problem, as opposed to someone saying, 'Isn't this great. What can we do to support this?'" (Support worker in day service)

A minority of staff questioned if work in this area was a realistic possibility. For example, a health promotion worker had attempted to find staff in other services for us to interview, but without success:

"I have brought your information along to a meeting where we were discussing personal relationships for people with learning disabilities and right at the end people were sort of, 'Hah, this is not going to happen here. It would be great but let's be realistic about it.' And people were quite ... the feeling was that it is so difficult to broach the subject of heterosexual relationships, that to do the same-sex relationships would be inconceivable nearly."

Sometimes staff revealed that same-sex relationships were not treated with the same respect as their

heterosexual equivalents would be. People with learning difficulties often moved house without intimate relationships being considered. Staff in one service told us that two men had been in an established relationship in a residential home. However, when the time came for them to move on, the relationship seemed to be regarded by some residential staff as trivial:

"'Oh, those two just fondle each other in the toilets', kind of thing, rather than being taken with the same respect and seriousness as a heterosexual relationship would be." (Manager in a residential service)

But other staff interviewed had played a more supportive role. One housing officer had challenged the attitudes of other staff when he was involved in rehousing people with learning difficulties, who were moving out of hospital. He told us about two women he had worked with:

"They wanted to live together and there was a lot of confusion about why they actually wanted to live together. But my role was to go out to see them, to look at this set-up, the community set-up for them. Both the house itself and the furnishings to make that home for them. Within minutes of actually sitting down with them, they were very clear about going through each of the rooms, and we got to the bedrooms, they automatically identified a double bed for them, and that was something so important to them because they identified themselves as a couple living together. During the discussions about that the professionals ... didn't sit very comfortably, because they were either naively unaware, chose not to be aware, chose to ignore it or something else. At the end of that meeting when the customers in question left, I was questioned about the clients and I said, 'Well, these people are customers or service users that we need to support', and I was questioned about the fact that I fully acknowledged their desire to fully live together and set up that house together as a living couple, which was now of concern."

Some staff reported the difficulties they had encountered when they wanted to introduce images of same-sex couples into their work or environment. Images of same-sex couples were viewed as problematic by some services. The trustees of a self advocacy organisation objected when pictures of same-sex couples were put up.

However, the chief executive had taken a stand and said that it was an equal opportunities issue and the pictures should not come down.

A member of staff in an FE college carried out an 'image audit' of posters and pictures around the building. She found many that depicted men and women together as couples, but no images of same-sex relationships. Her idea was that by having some images on display, they would "drip into the psyche of the place". She obtained some photographs from a couple of charities and her colleagues were supportive. However her manager had reservations and in the end the photographs were not allowed to be displayed:

> "I mentioned it to our site manager and she was really against it. And her words were that she didn't want parents coming into the site and seeing these images. I was quite shocked ... really angry at the time."

Pictures and images can convey an important message. They are a way of saying things about an organisation and saying to people with learning difficulties that things are OK and they are acceptable. However, finding useful images, especially of lesbians, can be difficult:

> "I mean, people don't have the image, if you like. You know, I think there isn't much around for women to look at and think, 'Oh yes, I'm like that'. Whereas you know now, there's quite a lot more on telly and so forth about gay men and things." (Support worker in day service)

Very little thought appeared to have gone into showing women and men with learning difficulties that a gay, lesbian or bisexual sexual identity was accepted within services. Workers at one sex education service, for example, had this to say about their visits to day centres:

> "You can see lots of different cultures represented, posters depicting Asian people, but there is never any kind of leaflets on gay helplines or posters promoting lesbian and gay pride.... I think there are very practical ways that people could show people that this is acceptable without having to get into a one-to-one discussion, trying to target potentially gay or lesbian service users."

Difficulties in accessing a gay, lesbian and bisexual scene and culture

Accessing the gay, lesbian and bisexual scene or social activities can be an important facet of accepting, and expressing, one's sexual identity. We saw in Chapter 3 that people with learning difficulties who wanted to do this were faced with a wide range of barriers. Staff in one service told us about one group of gay men with learning difficulties who went out as a group to gay bars. Transport was an issue in the way it often is for disabled people trying to organise social and leisure activities. Most of the men lived outside of the city where the bars were and most had to go home by 9pm, which meant that the bars were often quiet and so the opportunities to meet other men restricted.

This was also true for a gay man in another service, who lived with his mother. It was said that his mother did not like him to be out at night. While he had, with support, begun to access gay bars, he was only going during the day, when there were very few people there:

> "He lives with his parents. They are really restrictive with him and he doesn't get to go out at night.... They're very anxious about him going out at night. And he's kind of internalised some of that, so he gets anxious about night-times. But there's this real conflict going on inside him, because he wants to have a life and move away from home and have a relationship. But he's struggling with that, really, at the moment, because that's too much challenge to his parents. So he does everything in the daytime, so they've got no idea what he's doing in the daytime. So he goes to [gay pub] regularly and has a drink and goes there in the daytime, when there's not many people there and he just talks to the bar staff." (Manager in advocacy service)

In another service, attempts had been made to establish links with an organisation of gay men, which did not have an explicit remit around disability, but this had not been very successful:

> "It was sort of very body oriented and what you look like. If you've got a disability or look different or

something, that's kind of opposite of welcoming, isn't it?" (Development worker in advocacy service)

Many of the staff we spoke to thought of men's relationships exclusively in terms of having sexual partners. What was not routinely recognised by staff trying to support men and women was that there is a gay culture that people may want to find out about and have a choice about becoming a part of. As one support worker commented:

"I am working with a man at the moment who has a learning disability and he identifies as gay, but he is not looking for a sexual relationship at this time. What he wants is experience of a gay community and he wants to meet other men with learning difficulties, who feel the way he does. There is much more to his perception of being gay than just the sex, because that is not what he wants at the moment and maybe he will or won't in the future. But he wants more than that. He wants a recognition that this is part of him. This is part of a cultural identity that he wants to explore. To be part of that culture you have to be supported in it and you have to learn the codes and behaviours. You are not going to be able to enter that unless you have got support."

Cross-dressing

Several services told us how they had supported, or tried to support, men and women who were cross-dressing; that is men who dressed in women's clothing or women who dressed in men's. Staff brought this subject up with no prompting from us. They were frequently trying to find ways to support people who chose to do this. They were also questioning whether this meant the men and women concerned were gay or lesbian.

In one residential setting a young man lived in a small group house. His cross-dressing had made his housemates uneasy. A member of staff had negotiated with the group that the man could cross-dress in his bedroom but not in any communal parts of the house. We were told that the man was happy with this. This service, along with others, said that they felt isolated and unsure of how to respond to the situation.

In another interview, a tutor described her experiences with a student:

"One of my students was cross-dressing and coming in with bras on and ladies' underwear in general and was really starting to explore his sexuality. He doesn't speak but uses a series of gestures and he's actually quite expressive. And he indicated that he really fancied a male support worker. He started to share it with the other students and he was really chuffed and excited about doing that."

A sex education service involved in the research had also found itself supporting people who chose to cross-dress, as the services supporting the people directly felt unsure about doing this:

"Trying to get support for a man who cross-dresses to go to a bar ... at the end of the day we couldn't get somebody. It would have been great if we could have got a man who cross-dresses himself, who is familiar with the needs of people with learning disabilities, could take this man along to this bar and introduce him to this whole cultural experience. In the end, who did it? Us. And it was a bit like, 'Why can't you do it?'"

Staff at the sex education service were concerned that this visit was a one-off, and that the service was not funded for ongoing support of this type:

"I had to say to this chap, 'Well I can only do it once, just to give you an idea of what it is about'. Because he had never been to one and that is what he wanted to do, to go and see it. The benefit, really, is seeing that other people felt the same way as he did and it was to a degree acceptable and there were actually public places where people could cross-dress and, in that way, it was beneficial."

Supporting and sustaining same-sex relationships and sexual identity

One point that was common to nearly all of our interviews was a concern or frustration that any support given to people with learning difficulties would have a 'dead end'; that despite any support that could be given, people's ultimate goal of a relationship was unlikely to come to fruition:

"You can't, you know, you can't go that extra bit and sort of ... you know, because they come to that point where they actually say, 'Look, I'd really like to do something about this'. And it's not in my role in an educational environment to do very much about it. And he lives at home with his mum and you couldn't see it going very much further." (Lecturer in FE college)

Even where gay men *were* being supported to access the gay scene, staff said they were frustrated that things only went so far:

"I think what it's good for is that they're going to an environment where there's other gay men, you know, and it's strengthening their identity. But what it isn't really doing, I suppose, is they're not moving on. I mean, whether they should or they shouldn't, I don't know, but they're not moving on from that. It's just, you know, they go to the bar and have a drink and go home again." (Support worker in advocacy service)

One service felt that a gay service user would have more opportunities for relationships once other areas of his life had been sorted out, especially the opportunity for more independent living. They were putting him in touch with a citizen advocacy project, so that he could get control of his money and live independently of his parents.

Another service that had supported a man to use gay clubs and pubs, told us that now he wanted:

"... to meet people and from that friendships may come. And that being the main thing, not just being about finding a boyfriend, although that's his ultimate aim, he also wants gay friends so that he can talk to people." (Development worker in advocacy service)

Staff in another service told us about one woman who was very clear about what she wanted:

"She seems very open about talking about sex, one of the most open people about it. In a quite positive way, about enjoying it and having dreams about the woman she's got a crush on, taking her away for a romantic weekend and having sex together. Which is like really refreshing in some ways. It's a very positive image of sexuality for her. But she doesn't get to act it out in any way." (Training officer in advocacy service)

One self advocacy organisation had decided to develop a friendship group for people with learning difficulties who were gay, lesbian or bisexual. The group was made up mostly of men. Only one woman had attended. Although she was linked into other groups of non-disabled lesbians, she wanted the opportunity to be part of a group of other people (including women) with learning difficulties. However in the absence of any other women in the group, she had stopped attending.

Some staff reported on past, and current, experiences of successfully working with, and supporting, men and women who wanted to have, or were having, same-sex relationships. One service had organised a social group for gay, lesbian and bisexual people with learning difficulties. Another service was used by two young women who were in an established relationship. The relationship was said to have had a very positive impact on the service itself in that gay and lesbian social venues were now included in the social programme for the whole service.

In the same service, a gay man was supported by a non-disabled gay man from an external organisation to attend a drop-in group for gay men who were recently out, or thinking about being out. He had also been given support to travel to a larger city during the day to visit a number of gay bars.

In another day service, a support worker had supported one man in particular who had been identified as at risk because of his attraction to male members of staff. The staff member had looked for local support services but had not found any. Conscious that she was a woman and feeling that support from another man would be beneficial, she secured funding from the local authority to buy sessions for him with a private sexual health counsellor.

A residential service told us about supporting a man who identified as gay. There had been a lot of thought and discussion with him on the ways he wanted support. This has meant that customary working times for staff had been challenged:

"So for this guy that involves going to clubs twice a month till 3am, pubs Friday night till half 11. So then it's not your traditional early/late business at all, but the hours are just exactly what individual tenants need them to be, based on their lifestyles and what they want to do." (Support worker)

The manager of this service had asked for advice on supporting the man from an organisation recognised nationally for their sex education work. He told us about the information he had been given:

"Having a really clear support plan with really clear guidelines of how to support him written down, so you know, you've got a manual, if you like: how to support him in a night club, how to support him in a pub, how to support him when this happens, how to support him when that happens. That's hugely important. Checking out with the staff before they do a shift like this that they're happy to, and then obviously having a debriefing session afterwards and a lot of supervision of the staff who are doing that revolves around that. And then there's the issue of confidentiality, because while all staff need to know a certain amount of things about him, they don't all need to know the nitty-gritty details of exactly, 'Well, did he have unprotected sex or didn't he?' But he does have an understanding of who does need to know what, so again quite clear contracts and understanding of, 'Well, if you tell me this, I'm going to have to tell this person, but we won't need to tell anyone else'."

Homophobia and heterosexism

Negative staff attitudes towards same-sex relationships may be based on homophobic attitudes, that is, a prejudice/discrimination against gay, lesbian or bisexual people. The effects of homophobia on gay, lesbian and bisexual people can be profound (see Mason and Palmer, 1997). Heterosexism is a less used word and refers to the general societal assumption that everyone is heterosexual. Its effects can be just as disabling as homophobia. We came to see that both homophobia and heterosexism represented a significant barrier to both staff and service users who were in, or wanted to have, same-sex relationships.

The majority of staff we spoke to said that they worked in services and staff teams which were not homophobic, but which were fairly or very heterosexist. There was a wide range of responses to being asked about discrimination in services. Some staff and services said they were confident that they were not discriminatory. One member of staff in a day service, for example, was confident about the absence of either homophobia or heterosexism:

"Certainly within the staff team there wouldn't be any prejudice at all. I'm sure I can say that 100 per cent."

Indeed, some staff resisted the idea that homophobia was still an issue at all in society at large. One support worker, for example, suggested that there was widespread acceptance of gay men in society:

"Don't you think that you just see the person and think, 'Gosh I like him, he's a nice bubbly guy? It doesn't matter nowadays does it?'"

Elsewhere, however, staff did raise concerns about discrimination and its effects. Staff in one sex education service, for example, were very clear that homophobia prevented men and women with learning difficulties being supported on same-sex issues, but that it was not taken as seriously as racism, for example, in many services:

"There is just a general lack of awareness that this is a serous prejudice."

Some staff came out to us as gay, lesbian or bisexual themselves in our interviews. They reflected upon the common comment from heterosexual people in society that, "It's fine to be gay, as long as they're not in my face". We were told about this happening in services too. A training officer, for example, recounted the following incident where a course facilitator made a private remark to him about a gay member of staff on the course:

"There is a handful of gay guys [at work] and they are pretty overt about it. I was on a course last week with one of these guys and the facilitator said, 'If he goes on about his sexuality once more I am going to punch him'. Because, you know, some people do make a big thing about it."

Some gay, lesbian and bisexual workers saw heterosexism as a bigger problem with staff than homophobia:

"Everyone's so complacent, 'Oh I'm not homophobic'. But they're completely heterosexist here and they don't realise it. And when you sort of query, you're again labelled as the one who's always 'going on'." (Support worker in day service)

Heterosexual staff rarely recognised that making statements about their own sexuality, generally through disclosure about their marital/partner/ parental status was a 'coming out'. A female member of staff told us, "No, we don't talk about our own sexualities". However, in a conversation about boundaries between staff and service users the same member of staff told us, "They'll just join in the chat in the office, you know, your boyfriend's name…. You know, they'll ask about him and how he is." Another worker talked about the continual dilemma of when/how to come out to new staff members and pointed out that for heterosexual staff there is no dilemma, "They don't have to come in and say, 'And by the way, I'm straight'."

A lack of awareness on the part of heterosexual staff of their own self disclosure is also revealed in the following extract. Here a female member of staff talked about one of her male students who had a learning difficulty. He had made a pass at another male student in a taxi. She had arranged a meeting with a male colleague (Tim) and the student to discuss what had happened:

Staff: "And both Tim and I sort of just listened really and … very, very clear that there was nothing wrong with what he was doing, but that this student had come to me and said that he didn't like it. And then, that was really good, because then we had the opportunity to talk about, well, how do you make advances that are appropriate, you know? And how do you form relationships – physical relationships with people, appropriately? And you know, for example, you know, if you share a flat, I sort of said I wouldn't snog my boyfriend if my flatmate was there, because she'd feel uncomfortable about it. And then Tim talked about how, you know, he probably wouldn't go up and hold the hand of his male friend if

he hadn't checked out first that that male friend would like it."

Interviewer: "Was Tim indicating that he was gay or …"

Staff: "No he just talked about … I think that self disclosure is something we really don't … we haven't done."

Interviewer: "But you self disclosed …"

[long pause]

Staff: "Yeah I did actually, yeah I did actually, yeah I did. Maybe … yeah I did. It's interesting because my colleagues are gay but don't ever bring that into…. And it's a really interesting point actually, because I've got engaged and I talk quite openly about my fiancé and my engagement and my relationship. I do, I do. Not over the top, but I do. And I do use self disclosure actually … having said all that."

Heterosexism seemed also to extend to the places that women and men with learning difficulties were offered by staff as possible social settings they might visit. By contrast, both advocacy services that took part in the research included gay and lesbian bars in their nights out:

"People quite happily take them to all the heterosexual venues out there, and they're not necessarily saying that they're heterosexual are they?" (Advocacy worker)

A number of gay, lesbian and bisexual staff told us that they had been challenged about their behaviour with gay, lesbian and bisexual service users. For example, it had been suggested that they might not be the most appropriate person to work with another gay, lesbian or bisexual person with learning difficulties. By contrast, in some services it was thought to be of added value to match a gay, lesbian or bisexual member of staff with a service user who was, or was thought to be, gay. An out lesbian member of staff in a day service told us of a complaint that had been made against her by a male service user. The service user had said that he did not like a female service user putting her arm around the female member of staff. The complainant also suggested that the staff member was putting her arm around the service user. The staff member commented:

"And so, you know, I took that as being fairly homophobic in that, you know, I get attention all the time from men in the centre, you know, like smacking my bum or giving me a cuddle or kissing me. Anyway this incident was taken further. My manager picked up on it and brought me into the office and said, 'I need to act on it'. And then brought this person in who made the complaint and got me to defend my role in it. I mean if I filled out a form and reported every time someone smacked my bum, I'd be forever filling in forms."

Some staff talked about the very positive difference it had made to have gay, lesbian and bisexual colleagues. Organisations with gay staff, out or not, were often at the forefront of innovative work in this area. In one service, a member of staff said that it meant that it was harder to be reactionary than forward looking:

"I think if you challenged doing the work you'd have more trouble.... You know, it's the opposite here, it's like, 'We must do things more and more cutting edge, we must think about things'. And having a worker who's a confident gay man is a very positive image, isn't it, I think."

Sometimes there was an expectation that the gay, lesbian or bisexual member of staff would have a monopoly on expertise and skills in the area of sexuality and be willing to talk about their (personal) lives, without thinking through the approach of the service overall:

"I think sometimes the emphasis is put on lesbian and gay staff to do that, without a thought being put into what environment needs to be created to enable them to do that." (Support worker in day service)

One female worker felt that her service saw her as completely defined by her lesbian identity. This had proved too much in a service that she had previously worked in:

"It's quite clear through a number of the team members that actually I just became a member of staff who had a girlfriend and everything else was

irrelevant and it really negated the work I did. And in the end that's part of the reason I left."

Gay, lesbian and bisexual staff were often uncertain about being out at work and not confident that their workplaces would be accepting. A lesbian worker in a day service said she was out to colleagues and service users alike, but felt quite isolated as the only out member of staff:

"I'd say it's a hugely heterosexual environment, it really is. You know, and we're not doing very much to challenge that, I don't think. And I feel very alone in challenging that as well, you know, not particularly confident in sort of taking it on myself, you know."

One day service manager recounted how a lesbian member of staff had been told *not* to come out to a woman with learning difficulties, whom some people thought might be lesbian:

"It was said to her, 'Don't tell the lady as she'll make an issue of it'. And I thought, 'Well, if she ever wanted to talk to someone, there's someone there who maybe she might be able to just open up a little bit to.'"

One bisexual worker talked at length about how the teams she worked with did not value her sexual identity, nor see that it might be a positive strength, when working with someone who might identify as lesbian or bisexual. She was debating coming out to a service user whom she thought would value not feeling alone:

"When I relayed it to the team it was all shock horror, 'I can't believe that you brought your personal life in! You shouldn't be disclosing that.' Whereas they disclose they're married by wearing a ring. They disclose they're Black by having black skin. They disclose they're a woman by appearing like a woman.... But I wasn't allowed to disclose that. It was seen as very unprofessional that I was bringing personal stuff to my job."

A gay man in an advocacy service said that he was not out to people he was advocating on behalf of and explained why this was:

"I think I'd just feel quite exposed if I was, kind of, to just come out as a gay man working with them, really, in terms of harassment in language and stuff. And I guess that that's my experience of working with people in the past, where I feel more comfortable challenging something but not from a personal point of view, which kind of makes me vulnerable."

One senior manager in a residential service said that he was now out to everyone, including service users, because he felt his seniority protected him from allegations or negative feelings from other staff.

Professionals in Northern Ireland told us that it was generally unsafe to be out in almost any professional, or indeed personal, context. A support worker there said:

"I would say that this is not a safe place to be gay. There are very black and white ideas about sexuality. I think people would feel unsafe in terms of fear of being shunned. I'm sure there are people who have been given a good hiding."

Challenging homophobia and heterosexism

We were not aware of any research that looked at levels of homophobia among people with learning difficulties, but there is no particular reason to believe that they would be any different in this respect than the non-disabled population. We asked staff about this and there were mixed messages. In the main people with learning difficulties were described as being very open minded and rarely homophobic. However, a minority of people suggested that while people with learning difficulties did not discriminate in terms of gender or race they *were* homophobic:

"I've never come across a student discriminating against anybody else. And as soon as you put an image of a same-sex couple down it's suddenly this outpouring of phrases and words that ... I just don't know where they would have naturally come up with those words. It's almost like it's been said to them and they're just reflecting it back." (Lecturer in FE College)

Workers in a rural day service talked of how difficult it would be for a woman who seemed unsure of her sexual identity, as a man who lived in

the same house was very homophobic. The staff had challenged him gently on this, but felt that it was a losing battle as his parents were extremely homophobic. They thought this was where his attitudes – and reinforcement for them – came from.

In one day service, an openly gay man with learning difficulties had been challenging people's homophobic language. In a college elsewhere staff told us that they dealt with homophobic name calling by decisively telling students that it was not acceptable. The staff there found that:

"They [students] changed their behaviours because it was made very clear to them, it was explained very clearly, 'Well, actually, you just can't carry on coming if you do that in college, we just don't allow it'."

In a staff team supporting another openly gay man with learning difficulties, the manager was very aware that homophobia – on the part of the staff in this case – could be subtle. He noticed how some staff said that they were happy to support a gay man with learning difficulties at the same time as letting him know that they disapproved of his choice of gay venues. He said:

"You need to be really serious, making sure that the staff aren't giving out an unspoken message of disapproval at any point. And there was a couple of members of staff who I needed to speak to about that. Because while they were speaking the speak, saying, 'Yes, of course, we're really cool with doing this', some of the things they were actually saying were, 'Oooh, have you been *there* again?'"

Similarly, a lesbian lecturer at college noticed that when one openly gay student wanted to talk about his life:

"I felt quite a lot of homophobia from the staff actually, from the support staff workers in the group. It was like, 'Oh, don't say that', and, 'Don't do that'. More than the students – the students seemed to be quite accepting of him."

One manager of a number of services talked about the "well rehearsed norms of heterosexuality" in services. A worker in a day service said she felt that a Valentine's disco, where it was suggested that there should be a king and a queen, was the kind of thing she wanted to challenge.

Challenging heterosexual norms is not easy, Indeed it can be far less easy to do than challenging outright homophobia. A lesbian support worker said:

"I probably don't do as much as I should. But you know I'm out and I'm here and I do as much as I feel I can. I wouldn't say I was, you know, right up there fighting the cause sort of thing. But, you know, if it offends me or isn't inclusive of sexuality then, you know, I will raise that as an issue."

Summary

- *Staff experiences of gay, lesbian and bisexual people with learning difficulties* – The overwhelming majority of staff in the study said that they knew, or had known, men and women with learning difficulties who were having, or wanted to have a same-sex relationship. Staff said that feelings of guilt and shame had featured strongly in how the people with learning difficulties talked about their sexuality.
- *Privacy* – Staff were aware that there were few places where men and women with learning difficulties could go to have privacy together for intimacy and/or sex. There were particular issues about men in day services having sex with each other. Partly because of this lack of space, we were told about men using public sex environments, such as toilets.
- *Women's relationships with women* – Staff described women's intimate or sexual relationships with each other as largely hidden. Expressions of intimacy and touch between women were characterised as platonic and essentially unproblematic.
- *Attitudes of staff members towards same-sex relationships* – These were cited as a barrier to doing work in this area, as same-sex relationships were sometimes treated as lacking in value or meaning. While some services had been very thoughtful about their inclusivity and demonstrated this by including images of gay men and lesbians on the walls, others had faced opposition to doing this.

- *The gay, lesbian and bisexual scene* – We were told about difficulties for people with learning difficulties in accessing the scene. Gay venues were described as not particularly welcoming and access to transport and the views of parents and carers could be barriers. Little thought was given to the nature of lesbian, gay and bisexual culture.
- *Cross-dressing* – Several services told us about people with learning difficulties who were cross-dressing. Staff were not always sure how best to support people in this situation or what additional services or support were available or appropriate.
- *Supporting relationships* – There was some frustration from staff that they did not feel able to support men and women with learning difficulties to achieve their goal of being in a relationship. However, there were many positive examples of staff and services working in innovative and thoughtful ways to support people in this area of their lives.
- *Homophobia and heterosexism in services* –The majority of staff said that they worked in services and staff teams which were not homophobic, but which were fairly, or very, heterosexist. Heterosexual members of staff were unlikely to recognise that discussing their personal lives meant that they were routinely making a statement about their own sexuality. Some lesbian, gay and bisexual members of staff had been challenged about their interactions with lesbian, gay or bisexual service users. Most – but not all – gay, lesbian and bisexual staff were out to some colleagues. Services were generally described as "a hugely heterosexual environment". Very few gay, lesbian or bisexual staff were out to service users, although some were.

Conclusions

This chapter draws conclusions from our research findings and the stories and accounts that people told us. It returns to the question posed in the title of this report: do gay, lesbian and bisexual people with learning difficulties lead hidden lives? Are their loves secret?

Being and belonging: being gay, lesbian or bisexual and having learning difficulties

At the start of this research project, we tentatively talked about "same-sex relationships" instead of being gay, lesbian or bisexual because we were not sure how meaningful those words or labels would be to people with learning difficulties. In fact, the 20 men and women we met were quite clear that they were gay, lesbian or bisexual. This was an important part of their identity and almost all of them wanted to explore it a great deal more – mostly by meeting other people, but also by being able to go to more groups, events, pubs and clubs. It was interesting to note the way people in the study talked about "picking up" and "discarding" different labels and how people associated certain places and contexts with different aspects of their identity. Two men said that in gay bars they were "gay ... normal", and that they dropped their learning difficulty label – they felt they would do better in that space without a label that they felt stigmatised them. Several other people "put away" or hid their gay, lesbian or bisexual label, when they were with people, or using services, where they did not feel safe.

At the same time, Sean, for example, who had organised and was running a support group for gay, lesbian and bisexual people with learning difficulties, talked about why the group was set up just for people with learning difficulties, when he had been such an advocate for inclusion all his life. Sean's view was that people needed a safe space to get support to be more comfortable with being a person with a learning difficulty who was gay, lesbian or bisexual. The group existed, he said, partly so that people could get strength from one another, so that they had a better chance as individuals and as a group of 'taking on' discrimination and prejudice. Like anyone, people in this study found that they could forge different identities in different places as Williams (2002) also found.

Much of what people told us about their 'coming out', their developing sexuality and emerging sense of self is completely in common with the accounts and stories of non-disabled gay, lesbian and bisexual people. Yet we certainly did not hear about very many successful links into the non-disabled gay, lesbian and bisexual community. People with learning difficulties may need different and/or additional kinds of support to be able to meet people and lead sexual lives. Perversely, the reticence or ambivalence of many staff to support people in this area means that people with learning difficulties are given an even harder task when it comes to seeking same-sex relationships than their non-disabled peers.

Surviving and surpassing: stories of success

Many of the messages from the women and men with learning difficulties we interviewed were negative and difficult to hear. But what we hope is clear is that people's stories were predominantly ones of strength, survival and success. Despite the very many messages telling men and women with learning difficulties that it is a problem for them to be sexual at all – never mind gay, lesbian or bisexual – the people we met were forging their lives and identities and striving to lead full sexual and emotional lives.

Some of the people who were being most successful at making links into gay, lesbian and bisexual communities were members of self advocacy organisations which tended to prioritise people's aspirations for leisure and social activities. Carson and Docherty (2002) suggest that staff in services like day centres and residential settings may not be best placed to advocate for, or support, people with learning difficulties around friendships and relationships. They suggest that in addition to self advocacy, citizen advocacy may be a more productive source of support.

Love, actually: what do women and men with learning difficulties want from relationships?

Conversation about love ran throughout the core of our interviews with women and men with learning difficulties. It seems important to us to highlight this and to make what again might seem like an obvious point, that love mattered a great deal. This was clear to the college tutor we interviewed, who thought it made no sense to leave relationships out of her life skills curriculum and also to the self advocacy organisation that had decided to prioritise leisure and social activities above all else to meet people's stated needs around friendships and relationships. Talk of love led to the most animated part of our interviews with men and women with learning difficulties. Sometimes there was a deep and profound sadness at the absence of it, a frustration at the barriers that

seemed to be in the way of finding it, or the complete and utter joy of experiencing it – in all its guises: Angelique and Sarah wanted to marry each other and live 'happily ever after'; Robert wanted to meet a man who liked the same kind of music as he did; Jim wanted to be able to go cruising at his leisure without interference; and Ann wanted, more than anything else, to meet another lesbian to talk to.

Implications for policy, staff and services

This report concludes with a series of suggestions and recommendations for services about how they could support men and women with learning difficulties in this area of their lives. Overall, our findings would suggest that there are clear messages for staff and services about 'what works'. Staff doing the most developed work in this area felt confident, had policies and training, the support of managers and had thought about equality and diversity issues. In turn, people with learning difficulties said that what made a difference were open and non-judgemental staff, services that felt accepting, practical support to achieve goals – especially meeting other people – and images and pictures which made it "OK to have anyone you love", as Paul said. Jim told us that he came out because he went to a service that made him feel that it would be OK to do that. In the end, seeing a picture of two gay men helped him to come out and talk about parts of his life he had never spoken about before. It changed his life.

The reticence of many staff to discuss sexuality, and especially to discuss gay, lesbian and bisexuality, needs unpicking. We heard staff tell us that it was empowering to let people bring up issues themselves and that it was desirable to treat everybody the same rather than focus on differences in sexuality. Our findings suggest that the problem with treating everybody the same is that this tends to mean treating everybody as heterosexual. And meanwhile, people like Stephen and Mark feel that it isn't OK to be gay at college or at the day centre because they don't know "what staff will think" or whether they will be asked to leave. Writing about issues for Black and minority ethnic disabled people, Flynn (2002) writes that:

> ... agencies are unlikely to be inclusive if they fail to acknowledge different needs and insist that they 'treat everyone equally' without examining what this means.

The message for social policies seems to us to be about recognising that people's emotional and sexual needs are just as important as, if not more important than, their housing, employment or general health needs. Is it because people with learning difficulties are felt to be so behind the general population in gaining access to a place to live, a job and so on (Turning Point, 2004) that love, sex and relationships are the 'icing on the cake', for some time in the future? Shildrick (2004, p 154) argues that once the connections between sexuality, body, identity and discrimination are recognised, then:

> ... social policy has a high responsibility, as much ethical as practical ... social policy requires a greater sensitivity to all the different needs *and* desires of disabled people. (emphasis in original)

In Chapter 3, Stephen told us that staff needed to accept their professional responsibilities to support him, or get another job. This is a robust challenge to staff and services. We interviewed staff who recognised the need to develop better practice in this area a long time ago and who were doing outstanding work. We also met other staff in other services who were not. A sobering statistic, which underlines the scale of change that is required, is presented in research by Clarke and Finnegan (2005) into the Human Rights Act and its relevance to people with learning difficulties. They found that while 76% of staff interviewed said that they would support a person with a learning difficulty to develop a heterosexual relationship, only 41% said they would do the same for a same-sex relationship.

Secret loves, hidden lives?

We met and spent time with 20 women and men with learning difficulties who were gay, lesbian or bisexual. Were their loves secret and their lives hidden? Yes and no. It was difficult to find nine bisexual or lesbian women with learning difficulties to interview across the whole of the UK. There have to be more. We could have quite easily involved another 10 or 20 gay men with learning difficulties. Women's relationships with each other seem to continue to be far less visible than men's. Susie said she knew other lesbians with learning difficulties who were "hidden away". Ann's long standing and highly developed yearning for sex with a beautiful, large woman had been shared with perhaps just one other person. At the time of writing, and four months after we met Pauline, she continues to telephone us and explore options for support, so that she can one day go to a pub she knows and talk to and meet another lesbian woman.

Jim's experience of a very hidden past love caused him untold anguish, Owen was keeping his sexuality a secret from all of his large family and Pauline thought she might lose her friends if she came out. In fact, almost everybody we met was keeping their sexuality hidden from some very significant people in their lives for fear of rejection or prejudice.

Less hidden were people like Sean, Sally and Stephen who were setting up support groups and considering options around advocacy projects for other gay, lesbian and bisexual people with learning difficulties. Angelique and Sarah could hardly be more out as a couple and Mark had the complete and proactive support of his family who drove him to meet us for his interview.

The other things that have been hidden and secret until now are people's stories themselves. The telling of them seemed to have a profound effect on many of the people whom we met. They had a huge impact on us as researchers. We hope they will be significant to people who read this report, as well.

7

Recommendations

In this chapter we outline suggestions and recommendations for supporting people with learning difficulties in the area of sex, sexuality and relationships.

Approaching work on sex, sexuality and relationships

1. Be proactive in offering people opportunities to reflect upon, and discuss, their needs and wants in relation to sex, sexuality and relationships. The danger of *not* doing this is that men and women with learning difficulties may think it simply is not OK to bring up these issues.

2. Think about sex education as a human right that is essential to help people develop and be less vulnerable in a really crucial area of their lives.

3. Do not make assumptions about people's sexual preferences. Be open and non-judgemental about whatever people express – unless it is illegal.

4. Engage with people's parents/carers/significant supporters whenever possible and with the express permission of the person. Allow discussion about sex and sexuality to happen over time and be prepared to hear arguments you may disagree with. Listen to people's views and show that you are listening. Show that your concern is for protection through education, rather than vulnerability through ignorance. Be clear that the person with learning difficulties is your priority, and their rights are your job.

5. See sexuality in general as a priority. This means expecting person-centred plans to include sexuality issues. Sexuality should mean the breadth and richness of physical, emotional, intellectual and social relationships, not the narrowness of just the physical. Demonstrate that same-sex relationships are equal. Do this by talking about discrimination and homophobia and challenging it, where it arises.

6. Ensure staff and colleagues see it as their role to support the needs of the person with learning difficulties in this area of their lives. Provide them with training and back up to do so – or ask for it to be provided for you.

Training

1. Training should be readily available. It should be challenging but not set out to outrage or alienate.

2. Training should include work that encourages people to look at their own values. Look at what it means for staff to set aside deeply held beliefs if they conflict with the needs of the person they work with and support.

3. Training needs to be backed by policies around work on sex and sexuality, so that staff can put lessons from training into practice with confidence.

4. Training should be offered and encouraged around diversity issues in general to enable wider understanding of oppression and its effects.

5. Provide training for women and men with learning difficulties on homophobia and what it feels like to be discriminated against in this

way. Also provide training on organisational policies on equality and discrimination.

Policies

1. In policies on equal opportunities, sex or sexuality and relationships, emphasise that same-sex relationships should be respected in the same way as any others. This includes men and women with learning difficulties being able to go to gay/lesbian venues. Have an upfront statement about the value of same-sex relationships; ensure that they state that partners of gay men and lesbians should have the same benefits from the service as partners in heterosexual or married couples.
2. Refer to women specifically, to remind everyone that women have same-sex relationships too.
3. In policies, encourage staff to be proactive – sex education is a right. It should not be dependent on people knowing what to ask for or feeling it is safe to ask. Include an expectation that sexuality will be covered in a person's plan.
4. Ensure that the respectful culture demanded by an equal opportunities policy is part of the culture of the service and not just words on a piece of paper.
5. Talk with gay, lesbian and bisexual staff about whether they are 'out' to everyone in the service. If not, what makes it feel unsafe? If staff don't feel safe, then it is highly unlikely that women and men with learning difficulties will. What could be different to make it feel safer?
6. Find ways of making these policies part of everyday life: look at how they are being implemented in team meetings; look at individuals' difficulties in supervision; encourage the challenging of homophobic and heterosexist remarks. Undertake discussions or surveys of staff's experience of discrimination in the work place. Talk with women and men with learning difficulties about their experience of prejudice – including all aspects of equality, not just disability.
7. Ensure that men and women with learning difficulties are familiar with policies and involved in putting them together and that policies are available in accessible formats.

8. Identify a senior manager to take the lead on coordinating and implementing a sexuality policy and to monitor its impact. Staff training is not enough on its own to ensure that staff and services change in this area.
9. If a person with learning difficulties is out (either through their behaviour or words), it is vital that all staff working with that person are not homophobic. Ensure that questions around this are asked at interview and that this is an issue, along with heterosexism, that is talked about at team meetings and in supervision.
10. Failure to follow policies ordinarily constitutes a disciplinary offence. Services should apply these procedures consistently so that policies on sex and sexuality are not disregarded or flouted.

Supporting same-sex relationships

1. Challenge outright prejudice from people with learning difficulties carefully – it may be homophobia from a heterosexual person but it may also be homophobia from someone who is scared or unsure abut their own sexuality.
2. If services are saying that people have a right to be sexual yet do not provide private spaces for this, the unspoken message is clear: be sexual, but it's nothing to do with us and we do not want to know. Services need to consider whether it is possible to offer private spaces. If not, where can people go? Write this down.
3. Question whether men's same-sex relationships are 'just' sexual, or whether they would like any support to develop their relationship in other ways.
4. Think about women's close and intimate relationships with other women. Might they want them to become sexual, with support? Might they already be sexual?
5. Be careful not to fall into stereotypical expectations of people who want to use the labels of 'gay' or 'lesbian' – for example that gay men are camp and have many sexual partners or that lesbians have very short hair and only have one sexual partner.
6. Ensure that space is given for people to hear, use and understand the words 'gay', 'lesbian' and 'bisexual'. (Remember that sexual abuse

Jones, V. (1995) 'Heterosexism and homosexual oppression in the provision of services to support the sexuality of people who have a learning difficulty', unpublished BA dissertation, King Alfred's College, Winchester.

Keywood, K. (2003) 'Supported to be sexual? Developing sexual rights for people with learning disabilities', *Tizard Learning Disability Review*, vol 8, no 3, pp 30-6.

King, M. and McKeown, E. (2003) *Mental health and social well-being of gay men, lesbians and bisexuals in England and Wales*, London: MIND.

McCarthy, M. (1999) *Sexuality and women with learning disabilities*, London: Jessica Kingsley.

Mason, A. and Palmer, A. (1997) *Queerbashing*, London: Stonewall.

Mencap (1999) *Living in fear: The need to combat bullying of people with learning disabilities*, London: Mencap.

Plummer, K. (1995) *Telling sexual stories: Power, change and social world*, London: Routledge.

Scottish Executive (2003) *Enhancing sexual well-being in Scotland: A sexual health and relationship strategy* (www.scotland.gov.uk/ sexualhealthstrategy).

Shakespeare, T. (2000) 'Disabled sexuality: towards rights and recognition', keynote conference address, reprinted at: (http://bentvoices.org/ culturecrash/shakespeare.htm).

Shakespeare, T., Gillespie-Sills, K. and Davies, D. (1996) *The sexual politics of disability: Untold desires*, London: Cassell.

Shildrick, M. (2004) 'Silencing sexuality: the regulation of the disabled body', in J. Carabine (ed) *Sexualities: Personal lives and social policy*, Bristol: The Policy Press, pp 123-57.

Taylor, S. and Bogdan, R. (1984) *Introduction to qualitative research methods: The search for meaning*, New York, NY: John Wiley & Sons.

Thompson, D. (2001) 'Is sex a good thing for men with learning disabilities?', *Tizard Learning Disability Review*, vol 6, no 1, pp 4-12.

Thompson, D. and Brown, H. (1997) *Response-ability: Working with men with learning disabilities who have difficult or abusive sexual behaviour*, Brighton: Pavilion.

Thompson, A., Bryson, M. and Castell, S. (2001) 'Prospects for identity formation for lesbian, gay or bisexual persons with developmental disabilities', *International Journal of Disability, Development and Education*, vol 48, no 1, pp 53-65.

Turning Point (2004) *Hidden lives: Improving life chances for people with a learning disability*, London: Turning Point.

Williams, C. (1995) *Invisible victims: Crime and abuse against people with learning difficulties*, London: Jessica Kingsley.

Williams, V. (2002) 'Being researchers with the label of learning difficulty: an analysis of talk in a project carried out by a self-advocacy research group', unpublished PhD thesis, The Open University, School of Health and Social Welfare, Milton Keynes.

Appendix:
Resources and further reading

Aziz, R. and Alam, A. (2000) *Reach out: Training pack on personal relationships, sexuality and needs of African and Asian descent learning disabled women*, London: fpa (www.fpa.org.uk).

Burbridge, N., Howarth, J., and Prosser, D. (1997) *How to use a condom for men who have sex with men*, Hertfordshire: Consent (telephone 01923 670796).

Cambridge, P. (1997) *HIV, sex and learning disability*, Brighton: Pavilion (www.pavpub.com).

Clarke, S. (1992) *My choice, my own choice*, Suffolk: Concord Video (www.concordvideo.co.uk).

Craft, A. and Bustard, S. (2004) *Living your life*, London: Brook (www.brook.org.uk).

Fanstone, C. and Andrews, S. (2005) *Learning disabilities, sex and the law: A practical guide*, London: fpa.

Ford, H. (2002) *Emotional health and well-being: Challenging homophobia*, Newcastle: MESMAC North-East (www.mesmacnortheast.com).

Frawley, P., Johnson, K., Hillier, L. and Harrison, L. (2004) *Living safer sexual lives*, Brighton: Pavilion.

Gildersleeve, C. and Platzer, H. (2003) *Creating a safe space*, Brighton: Pavilion.

Hannah, A. and Stewart, S. (2002) *Equality, diversity, inclusion: Challenging homophobia*, London: fpa.

Howarth, J., Abbott, D. and Peters, S. (due summer 2005):

  1. Three photo-story booklets aimed at:
- gay and bisexual men with learning difficulties – focusing on messages from the research;
- lesbian and bisexual women with learning difficulties – focusing on messages from the research;
- men and women with learning difficulties – focusing on homophobia and discrimination.

  2. Staff training pack of photos of gay men, lesbians and bisexual people to explore stereotypes and prejudice.

Please check the Norah Fry Research Centre website for further details (www.bris.ac.uk/Depts/NorahFry).

McCarthy, M. and Thompson, D. (1999) *Sex and the 3R's*, Brighton: Pavilion.

Thompson, D. and Brown, H. (1997) *Response-ability: Working with men with learning disabilities who have difficult or abusive sexual behaviours*, Brighton: Pavilion.

Also available from The Policy Press

Making *Valuing People* Work
Strategies for change in services for people with learning disabilities
Rachel Fyson and Linda Ward

This timely report examines the strategic changes that are occurring within learning disability services as a result of the 2001 Valuing People White Paper. It offers evidence-based examples of good practice for all those involved in planning strategic changes to, or implementing change within, services for people with learning disabilities.

Paperback £16.99 US$28.95 • ISBN 1 86134 572 0 • 297 x 210mm • 96 pages • June 2004

Making a difference?
Exploring the impact of multi-agency working on disabled children with complex health care needs, their families and the professionals who support them
Ruth Townsley, David Abbott and Debby Watson

"The research is fascinating and there are many lessons to be learnt for services."
New Opportunity Newsletter (Handsel Trust)

Many health, education and social service initiatives aim to implement better multi-agency working between agencies and professionals. But what difference does this sort of organisational change make to those families and children on the receiving end? *Making a difference?* explores the process and impact of multi-agency working on disabled children with complex health care needs and the families and professionals who support them.

Paperback £14.95 US$25.00 • ISBN 1 86134 573 9 • 297 x 210mm • 96 pages • February 2004

Committed to change?
Promoting the involvement of people with learning difficulties in staff recruitment
Ruth Townsley, Joyce Howarth, Mark Graham and Pete LeGrys

Committed to change? describes the work of a project that aimed to put research findings directly into the hands of professionals and people with learning difficulties. The report shows how practitioners and service users can be encouraged and supported to put research into action and to use research evidence to improve practice and promote change within their own organisations.

Paperback £13.95 US$22.50 • ISBN 1 86134 434 1 • 297 x 210mm • 80 pages • July 2002
Published in association with the Joseph Rowntree Foundation

To order further copies of this publication or any other Policy Press titles please contact:

In the UK and Europe:
Marston Book Services, PO Box 269,
Abingdon, Oxon, OX14 4YN, UK
Tel: +44 (0)1235 465500
Fax: +44 (0)1235 465556
Email: direct.orders@marston.co.uk

In the USA and Canada:
ISBS, 920 NE 58th Street, Suite 300,
Portland, OR 97213-3786, USA
Tel: +1 800 944 6190 (toll free)
Fax: +1 503 280 8832
Email: info@isbs.com

In Australia and New Zealand:
DA Information Services,
648 Whitehorse Road Mitcham,
Victoria 3132, Australia
Tel: +61 (3) 9210 7777
Fax: +61 (3) 9210 7788
E-mail: service@dadirect.com.au

Further information about all of our titles can be found on our website:

www.policypress.org.uk